BUILDING AMERICA
THEN AND NOW

THE
HOOVER DAM

BUILDING AMERICA: THEN AND NOW

BUILDING AMERICA
THEN AND NOW

THE
HOOVER DAM

REBECCA ALDRIDGE

CHELSEA HOUSE
PUBLISHERS
An imprint of Infobase Publishing

The Hoover Dam

Chelsea House
An imprint of Infobase Publishing
132 West 31st Street
New York, NY 10001

Library of Congress Cataloging-in-Publication Data
Aldridge, Rebecca.
    The Hoover Dam / by Rebecca Aldridge.
        p. cm.—(Building America : then and now)
    Includes bibliographical references and index.
    ISBN 978-1-60413-069-0 (hardcover)
    1. Hoover Dam (Ariz. and Nev.)—Juvenile literature. 2. Dams—Design and construction—Juvenile literature. 3. Water-supply—Southwest, New—Juvenile literature. I. Title. II. Series.
TC557.5.H6A43 2009
627'.820979313—dc22   2008025545

Text design by Annie O'Donnell
Cover design by Ben Peterson

Printed in the United States of America

Bang NMSG 10 9 8 7 6 5 4 3 2 1

This book is printed on acid-free paper.

CONTENTS

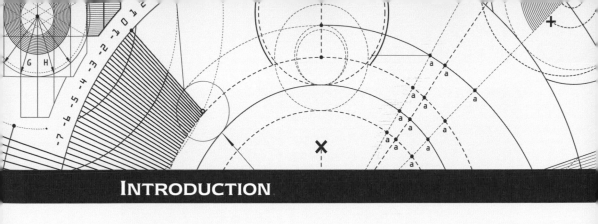

The Dry West

The time was the early 1930s, the president was Herbert Hoover, and the situation in the United States looked bleak. The stock market had crashed in 1929, and most Americans were hurt by the Great Depression, which left a majority of them jobless, homeless, and penniless. But in the West, a beacon of hope was in the works—a major structure that would symbolize the nation's technological prowess. That structure, built as graceful as it was strong, would come to be known as the Hoover Dam.

In the dry western United States, water resources and water rights had almost always been an issue. For this growing area of the country, water for drinking and irrigating land was an ever-increasing necessity. The United States Reclamation Service was formed to help deal with these concerns. This government entity and its engineers would come to play a great part in the construction of the Hoover Dam.

When early settlers arrived in the West, they could hardly have been able to imagine that any structure could control the Colorado River and its strong-minded flow. Yet a man named

The Hoover Dam *(above)* was built to provide the western United States with water. Although it was a dangerous and risky venture, the construction project created jobs for thousands of unemployed men during the Great Depression. Located on the Colorado River, this ambitious feat of engineering is one of the largest hydroelectric projects in the history of the United States.

Arthur Powell Davis dreamed an amazing dream for the area of the Colorado Basin. Davis's dream certainly did not become a reality overnight. For a project of this magnitude to succeed, field investigations would have to be conducted, politicians would have to organize, seven western states that had been arguing for years would have to make a final and lasting negotiation on water rights, and a company that could actually bring to life such an enormous entity would have to be found. It took years, but eventually all obstacles were overcome.

Created from a whopping 4.5 million cubic yards (3.4 million cubic meters) of concrete, the majestic dam was built in the middle of nowhere, stretching across the mighty Colorado River in the desolate Black Canyon. To provide for the dam's construction, the government would have to lay down rail line, electricity would have to be connected, and living quarters for thousands of workers would have to be built. In short, the dam was an immense undertaking.

The organization in charge of building this one-of-a-kind dam from the canyon floor up was Six Companies—a conglomeration of several businesses and individuals with construction and engineering experience who could not possibly have done the job alone. The ones responsible for its actual rise, block by block, 726 feet (221.3 meters) into the air were 5,000 men who came from all across the country. Most of these men were desperate to feed themselves and their families in the hungry times of the Depression. Living and working in extreme conditions, these workers—some with no previous construction experience—jackhammered, blasted, dug, and swung hundreds of feet in the air from the canyon walls, all in the name of progress.

Over the course of several years—from 1931 to 1936—the dam took shape, a reservoir was created, and a hydroelectric power plant was built. During this time, the construction claimed 96 lives. In the end, however, this fascinating superstructure—and the world's tallest dam at the time—would prove to be a lasting memorial to the thousands of men who saw it to completion.

Although the Hoover Dam has since been surpassed in height, it remains one of the most widely recognized structures in the world—and a crowning achievement in American engineering.

CHAPTER 1

Before Hoover Dam

Dams—the kind made by humans—date back thousands of centuries, but beavers are likely the ones to thank for this development in civil engineering. These hardworking, furry critters were the first to build dams. Their handiwork may well have provided the inspiration early humans needed to embark on the ambitious goal of controlling a river's flow.

DAMS AROUND THE WORLD

Dam building was an important development in civil engineering that progressed around the world and through the centuries long before the Hoover Dam was built. From Egypt to Mesopotamia to Europe, people discovered that dams could irrigate dry lands, provide water for drinking, and even create a beautiful lake for pleasure and recreation.

Egyptian Dams

The world's earliest dams appeared in lands where the climate was particularly dry. The single-earliest-known dam was the Egyptian dam Sadd-el-Kafara, the remains of which were found in 1885 by German archaeologist George Schweinfurth in Helwan, an area 20 miles (32 kilometers) south of Cairo. He and other experts estimated that the dam, whose name means "Dam of the Pagans," was built between 2950 and 2750 B.C. The dam, approximately 350 feet (106.7 meters) long and 37 feet (11.3 meters) tall, created a fairly large artificial lake, or reservoir. Considering the lack of technology available in ancient times, it may be surprising to learn that 100,000 tons (90,719 metric tons) of material were used to create Sadd-el-Kafara, one of the world's oldest civil engineering structures. Built in three sections, the dam's thickness was 276 feet (84.1 meters) at the base and 200 feet (61 meters) at its crest, or highest point. The early Egyptian builders also employed the technique of covering the sloping side of the dam—which was exposed to the river's water—with a limestone coating. This extra step protected the dam from erosion. As good as all of this may sound, the dam actually was poorly constructed and not watertight.

The majority of early dams were built to irrigate land, but experts think the Sadd-el-Kafara was different. Archaeologists believe its main purpose was to provide drinking water for both people and animals. Unfortunately, the dam did not serve the people of Egypt for long; most likely, a flood destroyed it only a few years after its completion. Experts were aided in this conclusion by material the dam left behind. Silt collects and builds up in the reservoir behind a dam. In this case, experts could tell how long the dam was in use by the amount of silt they found behind it.

The Sadd-el-Kafara Dam was Egypt's first, and other dams were not constructed there until eight centuries later. Perhaps the failure of this early dam discouraged further construction attempts. Another explanation may be that there simply was no need for more dams.

Mesopotamian Dams

Mesopotamia was another site of some of the world's earliest dams. Although no physical evidence of dams has ever been

Beavers living around small creeks build dams *(above)* from sticks, mud, and stones to create large ponds of water. Their ingenuity most likely helped provide the inspiration for humans to construct dams for purposes of irrigation, flood prevention, and energy production.

found in the region, ancient records prove they did exist—mainly in the many mentions of irrigation. A tablet discovered and dated around 2140 to 2030 B.C. refers to the wages women earned for using reeds to make a dam. More proof of the existence of dams comes from information on King Hammurabi, who ruled in Babylon around 1800 B.C. Hammurabi insisted that his people follow rules and regulations when it came to operating the numerous dams and canals attached to his many irrigation projects. According to the book *A History of Dams* by Norman Smith, Section 53 of Hammurabi's legal code described harsh punishment for anyone who ignored the king's law: "If anyone be too lazy to keep his dam in proper condition, and does not keep it so; if then the dam breaks and all the fields are flooded, then shall he in whose dam the break occurred be sold for money, and the money shall replace the corn which he has caused to be ruined."

MAKING AN OLD DAM NEW AGAIN

Alacahoyuk is a town in Turkey with a population of 2,500 people. Since the early 1900s, archaeologists have been digging near the town to uncover an ancient royal city. In 2002, a team from a local university unearthed something unexpected—a 3,246-year-old dam. The dam was built by the Hittites, who ruled much of the Middle East between 2000 and 1000 B.C. With help from the government, the university team removed an astounding 88 million cubic feet (2,640,000 cubic meters) of mud that covered the ancient dam. Even more remarkable than that, the stone-and-clay dam that served the Hittites all those thousands of years ago has been brought back to life. Now restored, it serves the town's current residents by helping to irrigate their farmland. The reservoir holds 1.1 million cubic feet (33,000 cubic meters) of water, and its original purifying pool makes the water drinkable.

Roman Dams

The Roman Empire was vast, and within its territories—including parts of North Africa and the Middle East—many dams were built, some of them remarkably big. Within their own nation of Italy, however, today's historians and archaeologists are aware of only three dams built by the Romans. One of these dams was built at the direction of Emperor Nero during his rule (A.D. 54–62). The construction of this gravity dam occurred near the emperor's villa in Subiaco, Italy. Not only was it one of the first dams ancient Romans ever built, it was also the tallest, reaching a height of 131 feet (40 meters). The dam's record height remained unbeaten until 1594, when the people of Spain built the similarly rectangular-shaped Tibi Dam extending 151 feet (46 meters) into the sky.

Nero's desire for a dam was not for the usual irrigation purposes. Instead, he hoped to create a recreational lake for his villa. Like the Sadd-el-Kafara, this dam too lacked proper construction—its rectangular wall was built too thin. Despite its faulty design, the dam managed to last many hundreds of years until 1305, and it may have lasted even longer were it not for two monks. Stories report that a religious duo was responsible for its failure. The dam's recreational lake was flooding nearby fields, so the two men removed a number of the dam's stones to lower the reservoir's water level and save their land. The Subiaco Dam is also linked to the oldest known picture of a dam. A monastery close to the site is the home of a painting from 1428 that depicts a saint fishing near the dam.

European Dams and Modernization

After the Roman Empire fell, the building of large dams was rare. Not until shortly after the Middle Ages—when dams were constructed in Northern Europe—did dam building reemerge. Dams improved life for Europeans by providing water for villages, water-powered mills, and canals. One such structure was located near Toulouse, France, in a town known as Ferréol. King Louis XIV approved this earthen embankment dam and its accompanying canal to maintain the area's local water supply during the dry season. Designs for the Saint Ferréol Dam were drawn up in 1662, and construction began in 1666. Completed in 1675 and reaching a height of 115 feet (35.1 meters), it was taller than any other embankment dam in the world. In fact, 165 years went by before another embankment dam surpassed this height.

The true beginnings of dam modernization in Western civilization began in sixteenth-century Spain. The country's dry climate and limited water resources made dams a welcome innovation. The people of Spain constructed gravity dams, curved gravity dams, and arch dams. The Spaniards not only built these structures, they also captured on paper their ideas for dam design and construction. They are credited with the first-known manual that describes in detail how to build a dam.

The Industrial Revolution of the eighteenth century brought more dams as cities grew and new industries were developed— all of which resulted in a greater need for available water. During this time, in 1736, Don Pedro Bernardo Villa de Berry made his own contribution to dam development. This Basque nobleman wrote about the geometrical rules one should follow when designing a dam. His work led people to use more specific calculations and reasoning in dam building rather than rely on intuition alone.

More progress occurred in the nineteenth century, when power tools came into use. With this development, engineers began to study how to build better structures. During the 1850s, W.J.M. Rankine—a professor of civil engineering at Glasgow University in Scotland—was the first to show how science could be used to alter dam construction, resulting in improved and stronger designs. Stronger cements and reinforced concrete were created at this time as well.

DAM TYPES

Dams come in several shapes and a variety of sizes. Early embankment dams eventually led to the construction of other types of dams that could better serve the factors of various settings. All four dam variations take a different approach to how the dam's upstream face resists the water's force. All four have something in common too: They must be wider at the bottom, because of the intensity of the water pressure below. The four types of dams that exist today are embankment dams, gravity dams, buttress dams, and arch dams.

Embankment Dams

The first dams built were embankment dams. They are the largest dam type. Unlike the three other kinds of dams, which are made of concrete, embankment dams are made using natural materials such as earth, clay, sand, and gravel. To build an embankment dam, the material is piled into one great heap and heavy machinery—such as large rollers—presses everything together as tightly as possible. Because the resulting material is so dense, it becomes watertight. Next, an outer layer of stone, called riprap, is used to cover the dam. Embankment dams can also be constructed using masonry blocks or concrete. These types of dams are most effective when a tall dam of shorter length is necessary—such as a dam needed for a narrow stream running through a mountain gorge.

Occasionally, embankment dams are filled with rock or a combination of rock and earth. Appropriately, these are called rock-filled dams. They can be less broad in size than other embankment dams because of their heavier weight. Gaps may occur between the rocks, however, creating the need for a layer of clay or concrete to make the structure impervious to water. Embankment dams are the thickest of the four types; the concrete used in the other kinds of dams is heavier than an embankment dam's earth and rock. Embankment dams also are the most common type of dam built in the United States. The oldest embankment dam made of rock still in use today can be found in Syria. It stands 23 feet (7 meters) high and was built about 3,300 years ago in 1300 B.C.

Gravity Dams

The sheer weight of a gravity dam is what holds back a river's flow. On the upstream side, or the side that faces the reservoir and oncoming water, the gravity dam's wall is built straight up and down. On the downstream side, the wall is built to slope. The dam's base width is designed to be about three-quarters the size of its height. The gravity type is the best choice for a dam that needs to stretch across a wide valley.

Triangular-shaped gravity dams, which were developed by French engineer J. Augustin Tortente de Sazilly in 1850, are the modern type still used today. De Sazilly demonstrated during a lecture that the use of a triangular face was most effective in the construction of a gravity dam. Although de Sazilly is credited with this development in dam engineering, the use of this shape dates back even further. The builders remain unknown, but triangular gravity dams appeared about 100 years earlier in Mexico (with construction dates of 1765 and 1800).

The use of concrete in dam building was another step forward. Its first appearance was in the Boyds Corner gravity dam built in New York in 1872. The next innovation in gravity dams was the use of steel rods within a dam's concrete base to help anchor the foundation. When this method is used, a dam does not need to be quite as wide. The construction of gravity dams reached its peak in the 1960s, and they are no longer used to the same extent. One well-known example of a gravity dam is Grand Coulee in Washington State, which required more than 20 million tons (18.1 million metric tons) of concrete to create.

Buttress Dams

A buttress dam is not as thick as a gravity dam at its base. Its buttresses are perpendicular walls shaped like triangular wedges that support the main, straight dam wall and bolster its strength. The buttresses distribute the weight and pressure of the water. This kind of dam often is cheaper to build than a gravity dam. The use of buttresses dates back to the Roman Empire, when they were added to a dam to support walls that Roman engineers deemed too thin.

Arch Dams

The Romans are famous for the arches they designed into their architectural works. Therefore, it is not surprising to discover that they were the first to build arch dams. What is rather unusual, however, is that Roman builders rarely used this type.

The first people to follow in the Romans' footsteps and utilize the arch dam structure were Mongolians. One of their earliest arch dams can be found in present-day Iran. When built in A.D. 1300, it stood about 85 feet (25.9 meters) high and stretched across its river for 180 feet (54.9 meters). The Mongolians' second arch dam project—located in Kurit, Iran—proved to be a major success. Built 50 years after the original Mongolian arch dam, the Kurit Dam reached a height of 197 feet (60 meters). This remained the tallest arch dam in the world for more than 500 years, until the early 1900s.

Like embankment dams, arch dams are good choices when a high but narrow dam is required. The wall of an arch dam curves outward on the upstream side, and the weight of the water spreads around the arch's curve. The valley's sides then provide a solid foundation to support the dam against the water's force. Sometimes arch dams are constructed with several arches instead of just one; these are called multiple-arch dams. The dam's strength comes from its curved shape, and the walls can sometimes be as thin as 10 feet (3 meters).

Combined Dams

Dam types can be combined to create the best defense against a river's flow. One example of combined dam types is found in

Nigeria, where a single dam was formed by building an embankment dam at each end and a gravity dam in the center.

THE COLORADO RIVER

The might of the Colorado River is responsible for carving out
the vast and scenic Grand Canyon that many visitors love to
explore. Yet, in the 1700s, the area was largely unexplored and—
to most people—daunting. The river begins its winding journey
in the mountains of north central Colorado. It travels southwest
through the desert in twists and turns for more than 1,400 miles
(2,253 kilometers), where finally it empties into the Gulf of California. The first white people to see the Colorado were Spanish
conquistadors who came upon it in 1539. The reddish and dark
river—full of mud and silt—went nameless for more than 200
years, until 1776, the same year America's 13 colonies declared
their independence from Britain. That year, Spanish priest Francisco Garcés named the river Río Colorado. Six tributaries stem
from the river: Green River, Gunnison River, San Juan River, Virgin River, Little Colorado River, and Gila River. The Colorado and
the area surrounding these tributaries make up what is known as
the Colorado River Basin.

Following the Mexican War (1846–1848), Arizona, California, and New Mexico became part of the United States. People
began to think that perhaps the Colorado could serve the West
in the same way the Mississippi and Missouri rivers served
eastern parts of the country—as a means of transporting
commercial goods. The nation's War Department also began
to consider the Colorado's potential contribution as a means
of connecting its outposts in the remote southwestern United
States. In 1857, to help determine the feasibility of this idea,
the department ordered Lieutenant Joseph C. Ives to travel the
river. His purpose was to report on the Colorado's suitability
and potential as a route for steam ships to carry provisions to
the area's army forts.

BUILDING AMERICA NOW

THE SALUDA DAM
REMEDIATION PROJECT

The Saluda Dam is located in South Carolina. It was about 70 years old when the results of a seismic evaluation were released in 1989. Before the dam was built, an earthquake that registered approximately 7.4 on the Richter scale had hit Charleston, South Carolina. The 1989 report determined that, if a quake of such magnitude were to hit again, the result would be the liquefaction of the 1.5-mile-long (2.4-kilometer-long) and 211-foot-high (64.3-meter-high) earthen dam.

The solution engineers came up with was not to reinforce the dam itself but to create a new backup dam made of 1.3 million cubic yards (988,000 cubic meters) of roller-compacted concrete in its center. The dam would also need 3.5 million cubic yards (2.66 million cubic meters) of rock fill to create two 5,500-foot-long (1,676.4-meter-long) sections—one on either side of the dam's concrete center. To provide a proper foundation for the earth and concrete backup dam, workers had to excavate a large area at the toe of the present dam. During the early phases of construction, the reservoir's water level also needed to be lowered at a controlled rate to keep the current dam stable.

Some creative solutions were implemented during the backup dam's construction. One was the creation of an on-site rock quarry, which saved both time and money because it meant tons of rock would not need to be shipped in from various locations. Another was an innovative recycling idea—using 200 million pounds (90 million kilograms) of coal ash waste from a power plant in the concrete used to build the dam.

The project began in the fall of 2002 and ended in 2006. It was named the American Society of Civil Engineers' Outstanding Civil Engineering Achievement in 2006—an award shared with other major construction projects such as the Trans-Atlantic Pipeline, the World Trade Center Towers, and the St. Louis Gateway Arch.

The Colorado River *(above)* was recognized by the U.S. government as one of the most powerful and vital natural resources in the United States. Beginning in Colorado and running through Utah, the river is a natural border for Arizona and Nevada. The waterway also runs through the famed Grand Canyon in the southwestern United States, and has been used to irrigate local farmlands for centuries.

Ives departed in January 1858 with a crew of 24 men. They traveled north from Yuma, Arizona, on the aptly named steamboat *Explorer*. It was not an easy journey for the men. At one point, the ship became damaged after hitting a rock underwater. As a result, Ives had to continue a portion of his trip on a small wooden skiff. Despite the trouble encountered during his mission, Ives stated in his report that the Colorado River could indeed be used to ship supplies, but only as far as Black Canyon. The lieutenant's outlook on the rest of the river, however, was much bleaker. Ives wrote in his report, "Ours was the first, and will doubtless be the last, party of whites to visit this profitless locality. It seems intended by Nature that the Colorado River, along with the greater portion of its lonely and majestic way, shall be forever unvisited and undisturbed."

Trying to Tame the Colorado

The Colorado gets its heavy flow of water in the spring from snow melting in the Rocky Mountains, but this torrent usually dries to a thin trickle once summer arrives. The year 1901 saw the first human effort to gain control of the mighty river. In an attempt to help develop the area, a private company took on the job of building a canal that would reroute some of the water from the river's natural course. This was achieved by cutting an opening in the Colorado's western bank and putting in a headgate to divert the water's flow. A set of small gates and channels worked together to bring water into Southern California's dry Imperial Valley.

At first, this system worked well and helped to irrigate fields, making once barren land fruitful and bringing in thousands of new residents. Several years later—in 1905—disaster struck in the form of a heavy flood. The Colorado overtook the channel system and continued to overflow into the Imperial Valley for an entire year and a half. This continuous flooding destroyed most of the area's newly created farmland as well as many homes and businesses. It also created today's Salton Sea.

President Theodore Roosevelt had to step in; he ordered a bridge that would help dam the river. From the bridge, workers dumped large amounts of rock for seven straight weeks. By February 10, 1907, the river was back on its natural course. Unfortunately, this was only a temporary solution. Because of the several years of destructive flooding in California's Imperial Valley, people began to voice stronger demands for flood control over the great Colorado.

CHAPTER 2

Arthur Powell Davis's Great Idea

The Hoover Dam never would have become the awe-inspiring structure it is today were it not for the Bureau of Reclamation and the vision of one man—Arthur Powell Davis. Davis's fascination with the Colorado River led him to push for a dam that would have far-reaching effects for the people who lived in the American West.

WHAT IS THE RECLAMATION SERVICE?

As the American West was settled in the late 1800s, a need for water grew. Because the West is such a dry region, the need for irrigation—diverting water from rivers and streams to populated areas—grew as well. Water storage was also necessary; this would mean "saving" the runoff from rains and snows during wet seasons for use during drier periods. In the beginning, these types of irrigation and storage projects were funded privately or by individual states, but they often failed due to a lack of funds or poor engineering.

As a result, people became increasingly interested in having the federal government involved in such ventures. Hearing the cry of the country's western settlers, Congress passed the Reclamation Act on June 17, 1902. This act would provide for the funding and construction of needed dams, which would eventually be repaid by those who benefited from them and any accompanying irrigation networks. In those days, the term *reclamation* came from the idea that irrigation would help "reclaim" dry lands, making them usable for the people living on them. Therefore, irrigation projects were deemed reclamation projects.

In July 1902, the U.S. secretary of the interior established the U.S. Reclamation Service, in accordance with the Reclamation Act, which investigated possible water development projects in the western states. From 1902 to 1907, the Reclamation Service began approximately 30 projects, which were hoped to improve living conditions and increase settlement and economic development in the West. The agency underwent a name change in 1923, becoming the Bureau of Reclamation.

Reclamation Today

Today the Bureau of Reclamation is known for the various dams, power plants, and canals it has built since its inception—including an impressive 600 dams and reservoirs—in a total of 17 western states. It is currently the largest wholesaler of water in the nation, providing 31 million people with 10 trillion gallons of the much-needed resource. Reclamation irrigates 10 million acres (4 million hectares) of farmland that in turn produce 60 percent of the nation's vegetables and 25 percent of its fruit and nuts.

Through hydroelectric power plants, the bureau is also one of the biggest contributors to powering the West. Its 58 power plants produce 40 billion kilowatt hours each year—enough to keep lights on, computers running, and televisions turned on in 6 million homes. This makes the agency the second-largest producer of hydroelectric power in the western United States.

Because the western United States experiences low amounts of rainfall year round and has limited access to fresh water, local communities rely on irrigation and runoff systems for water. *Above,* water is delivered to local farmland in Colorado via an irrigation system.

The mission statement on the agency's Web site reads: "The mission of the Bureau of Reclamation is to manage, develop, and protect water and related resources in an environmentally and economically sound manner in the interest of the American public." In the spirit of this mission, the bureau is involved in helping people meet their water needs and learning to balance the competing uses for this valuable resource. The agency emphasizes water conservation, water recycling, and reuse. It also monitors and evaluates the dams it has created to ensure they do not pose a risk to the public, and it makes structural modifications when warranted.

ARTHUR POWELL DAVIS HAS A DREAM

The year 1902, which marked the beginning of the Bureau of Reclamation, is also the year a significant idea sparked inside the mind of a civil engineer named Arthur Powell Davis. A graduate of Columbian University in Washington, D.C. (which later became George Washington University), Davis was the nephew of John Wesley Powell, who had helped open up the West to homesteading and development through his explorations of the previously unknown and mysterious Grand Canyon and Colorado River in the 1860s and 1870s.

A popular topic of conversation among John Wesley Powell's relatives was his discoveries in the West, especially the gorges

MAJOR JOHN WESLEY POWELL

It is said that, even as a child, John Wesley Powell showed an extreme interest in the natural world. On his own, he studied botany, zoology, and geology and made many expeditions. One of these excursions was a solo trip in a rowboat from the Falls of St. Anthony to the mouth of the great Mississippi River—all at the age of 22.

Powell went on to become a major after several years of military service. The Civil War's outbreak spurred his military career, which began in 1860 when he joined the 20th Illinois volunteers. In one of the war's many battles, Powell lost his right arm. Still, on May 24, 1869, at the age of 35, Powell led an expedition of nine other men down the Green River in Wyoming that would bring him national recognition. The tumultuous three-month journey greatly affected the team of men. After just one month, according to the John Wesley Powell Memorial Museum's Web site, one of the crew members—an Englishman named Frank Goodman—said to the major, "I've had more excitement than a man deserves in a lifetime. I'm leaving."

By the time the group reached the Grand River that would take them to the Colorado, they had already lost one boat and were about to encounter even more powerful and intimidating rapids. As a result of the danger, three more men left the expedition. When Powell and the remaining five found along the Colorado. As a result, in 1902, Davis turned his attention and studies to the Colorado River. He mapped its mountains and deserts and measured the flow of its streams. His investigations brought him to a specific place—Black Canyon, a scenic spot where distinctively tall and grand walls of rock tower over the Colorado River, which enters from the southern tip of Nevada. It was here that Davis had a vision of a great dam. From this moment forward, the civil engineer spent the next two decades focusing his energies on making his vision a reality.

John Wesley Powell's geological survey team, 1871.

members emerged from the previously unexplored Grand Canyon and the Colorado River, they were hailed as heroes. Powell began giving lectures and eventually raised enough money for a second expedition in 1871 that resulted in a map of the area and scientific publications.

The Hydrographer's Beginnings

Davis was a well-respected and extremely competent topographer and hydrographer who had begun his career even before the completion of his civil engineering degree in 1888. With a bit of help from his famous uncle, he became an employee of the federal government, working for the U.S. Geological Survey as a topographer and hydrographer from 1884 to 1894. Davis earned a promotion in 1895 and became the hydrographer in charge of government stream measurement. Another key assignment came three years later, when he was chosen to oversee two high-profile hydrographic examinations. As chief hydrographer for the Isthmian Canal Commission, Davis helped to investigate the Panama Canal route. For several years, he also worked as the lead hydrographer for the Nicaragua Canal Commission, which was responsible for determining the feasibility of a U.S.-operated canal in Nicaragua. As part of this process, Davis and the other members of the commission carried out the most extensive survey of the San Juan River ever conducted, gathering and recording information on such things as river discharge measurements, rainfall, and geological formations.

Davis built up an impressive resume over time. He had worked for Powell's Irrigation Survey, which undertook the task of finding reclamation and reservoir sites in the American West. In addition, his knowledge and expertise were put to good use in the design and construction of numerous dams—Shoshone Dam in Wyoming, Arrowrock Dam in Idaho, Elephant Butte Dam in New Mexico, and Big Bend Dam in South Dakota—as well as a large number of smaller dams, tunnels, and irrigation canals. In his book *Hoover Dam: An American Adventure*, Joseph E. Stephens says Davis "was without question the world's leading expert on reclamation." Thus, it only makes sense that Davis, after some time as an assistant chief engineer with the U.S. Reclamation Service, was appointed chief engineer in 1906, and later the agency's director on December 10, 1914.

An Idea Becomes a Plan

All that time with the Geological Survey and Reclamation Service had made Davis a verifiable expert on the Colorado Basin, and while he was a supervising engineer in the Reclamation Service he envisioned an overall plan to develop the area he knew so well. He collected crucial data on the river and its course as well as potential dam sites; Davis believed in a future dam that would provide flood control, water storage, and power generation for the dry and arid West. In Andrew J. Dunar and Dennis McBride's book *Building Hoover Dam: An Oral History of the Great Depression,* Walker Young—who became the dam's chief construction engineer—talks about Davis's plan: "Dr. Arthur P. Davis, who was then the commissioner of Reclamation, got the idea that a large storage should be provided for the lower Colorado River near the point of use. So he originated the idea. I consider him the father of the Boulder Canyon Project."

Davis's plan moved closer to fruition in 1922, when Congress ordered the Interior Department (of which the Reclamation Service was a branch) to study the Colorado Basin and its possible development, including potential problems. The result was the massive Fall-Davis Report. Its hundreds of pages contained all that anyone could want to know (and more) on the hydrological and geological aspects of the Colorado River and its surrounding canyons. The report covered everything from temperature and precipitation data to current and future irrigation needs for the region. In essence, especially for the nonexperts, the report boiled down to one crucial nugget found on page 21, where it recommended that the United States government build a large dam "at or near Boulder Canyon" and recover the cost through the revenue that would result from selling the electric power the dam generated to ever-growing cities in the West.

The significance of Davis's work and this report was captured in a 1933 *Fortune* magazine article about the auspicious dam: "Boulder Dam became a local and then a national issue. It involved scores of prominent Americans in disputes political, financial, and technical. But in the jagged valleys of the Colorado or in Washington or anywhere else there was no dispute about one fact: Boulder Dam was fundamentally the conception of Arthur Powell Davis; it was everlastingly based on his monumental engineering report."

BUILDING AMERICA NOW

SANTA ANA RIVER PROJECT

In California, a rockfill dam that could last 350 years was needed to provide flood protection in the upper Santa Ana Canyon. The result was the Seven Oaks Dam, which achieved a height of 550 feet (167.6 meters), a length of 2,980 feet (908.3 meters), and a reservoir capacity of 145,600 acre feet (179.6 million cubic meters). It ranks among the 15 tallest dams in the United States. Overall, it took 38 million cubic yards (28.88 million cubic meters) of rock, clay, and soil placed into 10 vertical zones to make a rockfill dam this large. California land is well known for its many earthquakes, and the Seven Oaks Dam was built with that in mind. Not only is it big, it is strong and designed to weather earthquakes that rate as high as 8.0 on the Richter scale.

The Seven Oaks Dam is just one part of a larger project called the Santa Ana River Project. As part of this project, another smaller dam is also being constructed on the Santa Ana River, 40.3 miles (64.9 kilometers) downstream from its larger cousin. Not actually new construction, the Prado Dam—meant to protect California's Orange County—is an enlargement of a dam originally built in 1941 by the Corps of Engineers. With the new additions, the dam's original height will increase 28.4 feet (8.7 meters) to reach a total height of 594.4 feet (181.2 meters).

The two dams will work together. Early each flood season, the Seven Oaks Dam will be used to store runoff in its reservoir. This

Hoover Dam's Father Fades Away

Unfortunately, because of the poor handling of the Reclamation Service's finances, Davis either resigned or was fired from his position as head of the agency in 1923. Even after he left the Reclamation Service, Davis remained involved in projects that

water can then be released in small increments to maintain the water supply that flows downstream. In addition, any time a flood occurs, the Seven Oaks Dam will hold the water normally meant to run downstream toward the Prado Dam. It will store this water as long as the level in the Prado Dam's reservoir continues to rise. Once the danger of flooding has passed, the water being held at Seven Oaks will be released at a controlled rate. At the end of each flood season, the Seven Oaks reservoir will be drained and the Santa Ana River will once again be able to flow through the area at its natural pace.

The Hoover Dam cost a great deal of money in its day, and the price of dams has not changed much over the years. The budget for the entire Santa Ana River Project is $1.4 billion, and the Seven Oaks Dam alone will require a minimum of $366 million of that money for its completion. Even with the modernization of machinery and equipment, dam building remains a lengthy process. The contract for construction of the Seven Oaks Dam was awarded in 1994, and building began in May of that year. The dam was finished on November 15, 1999. That means this dam—which is smaller than the Hoover Dam—took about five and a half years to complete. Construction of the Hoover Dam's diversion tunnels started in May 1931, and work on the entire dam was completed in 1935—only four years later, which shows what a feat of engineering the Hoover Dam truly was.

Following in his uncle's footsteps, Arthur Powell Davis *(above)* used his skills to explore and map the Colorado River area for the federal government. He compiled his research and data into a report, recommending a dam be constructed in order to provide power and water to the region.

required his extensive hydrologic and civil engineering skills. He worked on projects such as the development of local aqueducts in California, and in 1929 he left the United States for two years to take a position as chief consultant for irrigation in Turkestan and Transcaucasia in the Soviet Union.

For a decade, the building of the Boulder Dam went on without him—Davis's contribution was lost in the fray of political wrangling that developed around the great dam's construction. By the 1930s, Davis—whose health was deteriorating—lived in California. Around the same time, the dam's name was changed from Boulder Dam to Hoover Dam, and Davis's own name, which had never really garnered much publicity in the first place, faded altogether from the memory of those involved in its construction. Yet someone must have remembered, because in July 1933, Interior Secretary Harold Ickes named the now 72-year-old Davis as the dam's consulting engineer. Davis's failing health kept him from any real fieldwork, and he died just one month after his appointment.

WHY BUILD A DAM?

Davis's vision ultimately provided four substantial benefits to the people of the Colorado Basin area and beyond: flood control, water conservation, a domestic water supply, and power.

Flood Control

Before the dam's construction, the Colorado River served as a water source for the farms of southern California and western Arizona. At times, however, the river that helped these areas thrive also brought devastation in the form of floods that could destroy crops and sometimes kill farmers by washing them away. The Hoover Dam would help humans to override nature by controlling such floods. In addition, the dam would help with silt removal by collecting it above the dam. In 1933, floodwaters and silt cost the Southwest's ranchers about $2 million ($28.5 million today) in a single year.

Water Conservation

At the time of the dam's inception, the Colorado provided irrigation water for 660,000 acres (264,000 hectares) of land. Springtime in the West sees plenty of rain, but summer, fall, and winter have much sparser precipitation. Building a dam would mean that water from spring floods could be stored for future use during the drier months of the year, helping to increase the

WHAT IS A HYDROLOGIST?

Water falls to the earth in the form of rain and snow; it collects in oceans, rivers, and streams; it soaks into the soil, and it evaporates into the air. These aspects of water's relationship with the earth are all part of hydrology—the study of the occurrence, distribution, movement, and properties of water. A hydrologist then uses mathematical principles and scientific knowledge to solve society's water-related problems. These problems may be related to quantity, or a lack of needed water, and to quality, water that may be available but not clean enough for human use. More specific examples of issues hydrologists may try to resolve include locating water sources for farm irrigation and working to control flooding from rivers.

principal crops of the area such as alfalfa, cantaloupe, lettuce, barley, corn, small fruits, and cotton. In all, it would mean five to seven times more water for the summer season, or irrigation for an additional 1.5 million acres (600,000 hectares), bringing the original 660,000 acres (264,000 hectares) of land the river irrigated to an astounding 2.16 million acres (864,000 hectares). At that time, the extra 1.5 million newly irrigated acres (600,000 hectares) would equal half of all the new land opened by the U.S. government's 29 irrigation projects.

Domestic Water Supply

The cities and towns of southern California, especially Los Angeles, made up the Metropolitan Water District. The group was quick to sign a contract for a billion gallons of water per day for household use at a cost of $250,000 ($2.8 million today) per year paid to the federal government. In addition, the district spent $220 million ($3.1 billion today) for an aqueduct to facilitate the water's use.

Power

Once there was a specific plan for a dam, the power plant that would help pay for its initial cost was designed to be the world's largest—capable of producing 1.8 million horsepower. The city of Los Angeles and the electric company Southern California Edison signed 50-year contracts with the government to buy the power the dam would produce. Both would then subcontract 79 percent of this electricity (an amount set by legal standards) to Arizona, Nevada, the Metropolitan Water District, and numerous small towns in California's valleys.

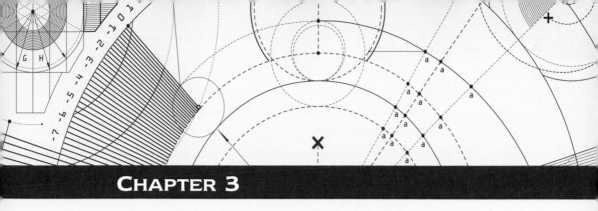

CHAPTER 3

From Idea to Approved Project

Arthur P. Davis may have had the idea for a great dam in the western desert, but a number of other men played significant roles in bringing the idea to fruition. In fact, several years of investigation and political wrangling took place before a specific plan for Hoover Dam was officially approved.

WALKER "BRIG" YOUNG

In January 1921, the U.S. Bureau of Reclamation initiated an official program to test the potential of damming the mighty Colorado. Walker Young, a reclamation worker since 1911, had significant dam-building experience under his belt when he was recruited to lead this mission by taking a team of surveyors through the Colorado River Basin. Young had helped with the construction of the Arrowrock Dam in Idaho. Now he was given the task of determining what area of the basin would best suit the construction of a large dam on the Colorado River.

The mission assigned to Young's team of 58 men was not without danger. They traveled each day on flat-bottom boats that they rowed themselves and camped on shore each night. At one point in their journey, a storm blew in that caused waters so turbulent the waves seemed more like those of the ocean than a river. Waves swelled so high that several men were thrown from their boats.

Eventually, however, the team's hard work and determination paid off. They evaluated several sites and submitted the results of their investigations. In the book *Building Hoover Dam: An Oral History of the Great Depression* by Andrew J. Dunar and Dennis McBride, Young explains one of the reasons Black Canyon was chosen for the dam site:

> The thing that turned the tide over was the fact that one day when I was trying to find out whether we could reach the damsite from the top . . . I discovered it was [possible] to actually build a railroad from the main line [in] Las Vegas to the top of the damsite. . . . There was considerable relief on the part of the chief engineer and his crew when we found we could get the resources, millions of tons of materials, down to that damsite on a standard gauge railroad. As I've said many times, the Lord left that damsite there. It was only up to man to discover it and to use it.

This investigation, and the selection of Black Canyon as the proper dam site, did not end Young's part in the creation of what would be the largest dam in the United States. In the summer of 1930, he was chosen as the chief construction engineer for the Boulder Canyon Project.

HERBERT HOOVER

Herbert Hoover was born in 1874 and became a millionaire before he turned 40 years old. He gained recognition for his efforts in relief work during World War I. Hoover, also respected for his skills as both a mining engineer and an administrator, gained political notice as President Warren G. Harding's choice

Herbert Hoover established himself as a man of action when, as the secretary of commerce, he surveyed the extensive damage in flood-stricken areas around the Mississippi River. Another major accomplishment during Hoover's service as commerce secretary was orchestrating the Colorado River Compact, a plan that designated portions of river water to each state in the region. *Above*, Hoover *(back row, left)* stands with flood victims.

for secretary of commerce. He remained in this role through Calvin Coolidge's presidency. In 1928, when Coolidge made the decision not to run for a second term, it paved the way for Hoover to become the Republican presidential nominee. Hoover had an easy win over Democratic nominee Alfred E. Smith and became the thirty-first president of the United States. In addition to his most famous role as U.S. leader, Hoover also was an integral player in getting the Hoover Dam built.

Man of the Environment

Hoover was a man with many interests. Aside from engineering and politics, he also had a love of nature; he was a fishing enthusiast and a conservationist with a deep interest in preserving the nation's natural resources. Just a year into his role as Harding's commerce secretary, Hoover was working hard to encourage other politicians' interest in topics such as flood control, fishery production, natural resource protection, and the cleanup of the country's rivers and harbors. To draw attention to these issues, Hoover spoke about them before Congress.

In part because of his relief work during the war, Hoover became known as "The Great Humanitarian"—but it was a situation in 1927 that really helped him to earn that title. That year, the Mississippi River destroyed thousands of acres of farmland due to flooding. Hoover visited the site of the damage almost immediately to see how he could offer help to the people affected.

Hoover was familiar with the devastation a mighty river could cause. As a California resident, he had taken many opportunities during the years before World War I to visit the lower Colorado River. So, a man of nature, Hoover was well acquainted with the problems the river had created over the years. Yet the engineer in him could also envision the river basin's potential for development.

THE COLORADO RIVER COMPACT

Legislation to approve the building of a large dam on the Colorado River was in the midst of being drafted in the early 1920s. At the time, Hoover served as secretary of commerce under President Harding. Also taking place during this period was a series of meetings to discuss water rights among the seven western states from which the Colorado River drains water: Arizona, California, Colorado, Nevada, New Mexico, Utah, and Wyoming. These gatherings of the states were Hoover's idea. The states in the region had been involved in long and ongoing legal battles with one another, so Hoover urged that a Colorado River Commission be formed to find a solution. The discussions that occurred during these meetings were often contentious, because each state had strong feelings about how to share the water fairly.

As the group's chairperson, Hoover met in January 1927 with state governors and other officials, and more meetings took place in various locations throughout the seven states involved. Next, commission members took part in an intense series of gatherings in Santa Fe, New Mexico. Here they spent 10 hours a day for two weeks trying to resolve the issue of water rights and the use of the river's flows. By the end of this 14-day period, nothing had changed. The states just could not agree.

Realizing the stagnation in their talks, Hoover—who had attended each and every meeting—came up with a plan of his own, trying to take each state's concerns into account. His idea became known as the Colorado River Compact. According to the plan, the water would be shared among the seven states, which would be divided into two groups—the Upper Colorado Basin and the Lower Colorado Basin. The Upper Basin states would consist of Colorado, New Mexico, Utah, and Wyoming. The Lower Basin states would include Arizona, California, and Nevada. Details of how water would be shared between the two groups were not finalized, but the compact was a good start. All the states except Arizona accepted the Colorado River Compact. Arizona's protest did not stop the compact from being signed by the six other states on November 24, 1922, finally ending the long-standing controversy of water division in the West. This compromise reflected well on Hoover, who was praised for the way he had handled the matter.

Even with this development, legislation for the dam's authorization moved slowly. Calvin Coolidge endorsed the legislation for the dam, but it did not have time to take effect during his presidency. On June 25, 1929, President Hoover signed a proclamation that made the Colorado River Compact effective. According to the U.S. Bureau of Reclamation's Web site, Hoover held a press conference that same day. Speaking to reporters, he said that the compact was "the final settlement of quarrels that have extended over 25 years . . . the most extensive action ever taken by a group of states under the provisions of the Constitution permitting compacts between states."

THE BOULDER CANYON PROJECT ACT

Congressman Phil Swing and California senator Hiram Johnson presented the Boulder Canyon Project Act in 1923. Their legislation, known as the Swing-Johnson Bill, was the first of three versions introduced between 1923 and 1926. Unfortunately, none of the bills was ever brought to a vote. In February 1927, the bill's third version made it further through the legislative process than its predecessors, but it still remained blocked from the voting stage. The bill was rewritten and submitted again in December of that same year. On May 25, 1928, it passed in the House of Representatives but was blocked in the Senate with a filibuster. However, at long last, during the Senate's second session beginning in December 1928, the Swing-Johnson Bill passed. President Coolidge signed the piece of legislation, making it law one week later.

Following the finalization of the long-awaited Colorado River Compact, President Hoover was able to sign a proclamation in June 1929 that made the Boulder Canyon Project Act effective. This action was the final authorization needed to spend $165 million ($1.9 billion today) on the much-anticipated Boulder Dam and its accompanying All-American Canal.

WHAT'S IN A NAME?

Before the Hoover Dam was constructed, when the idea for such a dam was in its early stages, the project was known as the Boulder Canyon Project. Even when it was finally determined that Black Canyon would be the optimal site, instead of Boulder Canyon, the people involved retained the Boulder Canyon name due to its familiarity. Once plans for the dam were made final, its official name became Boulder Dam.

On September 17, 1930, U.S. Secretary of the Interior Ray Lyman Wilbur attended a ceremony to mark the initial laying of railroad lines from Las Vegas to Black Canyon. At the ceremony, the interior secretary was to drive a silver railroad spike into the ground. W.A. Davis, who was living in the area at the time, recalled in the PBS film *American Experience: Hoover Dam,* "Secretary Wilbur drove the spike, he missed it about three or four times. And of course there was a lot of miners in the background to tell him what a poor punk he was. I think that he was quite embarrassed."

Yet this embarrassment was not what made headlines: It was Wilbur's address to the crowd that really caught people's attention. He announced, "I have the honor and privilege of giving a name to this new structure. In Black Canyon, under the Boulder

HOOVER DAM AT A GLANCE

★ It reaches a height of 726 feet (221.3 meters), which makes it 171 feet (52.1 meters) taller than the Washington Monument.

★ The top of the dam is 45 feet (13.7 meters) thick. The base is 660 feet (20.2 meters) thick, the equivalent of two football fields laid end to end.

★ The dam (including the power plant, intake tunnels, etc.) was created from 4.5 million cubic yards (3.4 million cubic meters) of concrete. That would be enough to build a two-lane road from Seattle, Washington, to Miami, Florida.

★ The dam's total weight is 6.6 million tons (5.9 million metric tons).

★ Each of the power plant's generators weighs 4 million pounds (1.8 million kilograms), about the same as four-and-a-half fully loaded airplanes.

Secretary of the Interior Ray Lyman Wilbur *(above)* traveled out West to drive the first commemorative spike marking the start of dam construction. At this ceremony, Wilbur announced the dam would be renamed Hoover Dam, after President Herbert Hoover.

Canyon Project Act, it shall be called the Hoover Dam." Herbert Hoover was president at this time, and Wilbur's boss. Wilbur went on to describe Hoover as "the great engineer whose vision and persistence, first as chairman of the Colorado River Commission in 1922, and on so many other occasions since, has done so much to make [the dam] possible."

A New Name Strikes Displeasure

The interior secretary's announcement met with little acceptance. Only seven months after Hoover's inaugural address, the Great Depression had struck. As president, Hoover declined to provide government assistance for all of the people who were struggling during the difficult economic times. Hoover's reasoning was that he did not want Americans to become dependent on the federal government for help. Needless to say, a large percentage of the American population was dissatisfied with his performance as the nation's leader. To them, naming the dam after Hoover was an insult.

Following Wilbur's declaration, the dam went by both names, depending on who was discussing the project. In the press, the name was used interchangeably; sometimes it was called the Boulder Dam, and other times it was referred to as the Hoover Dam. However, in any official documents, the name appeared as Hoover Dam. The naming controversy, however, was far from over.

Back to Boulder Dam

When Hoover lost the presidency to Franklin D. Roosevelt, Harold Ickes replaced Wilbur as the country's secretary of the interior. On May 8, 1933, Ickes made an announcement of his own: The name of the dam would officially revert back to Boulder Dam. According to the PBS *American Experience: Hoover Dam* Web site, Ickes said, "The name Boulder Dam is a fine, rugged,

(continues on page 48)

BUILDING AMERICA NOW

THE BIG DIG

When the Hoover Dam was built, it was the largest public works project ever undertaken; however, that record no longer stands. Boston's Big Dig now ranks as the largest public works project in U.S. history. What, exactly, is the Big Dig?

The project's official name is the Central Artery/Tunnel Project (CA/T). Boston's Central Artery highway opened in 1959, and back then it easily carried the 75,000 vehicles a day that rolled along its six lanes. Over the years, problems began to develop as the population and its use of vehicles increased. By 2000, stop-and-go traffic jams were happening for 8 to 10 hours every day. Use of the highway had risen from 75,000 vehicles a day to nearly 200,000. Experts projected that, if no changes were made, by 2010 the people of Boston would be sitting in traffic jams almost 16 hours a day.

Initial designs for the new construction began in the early 1980s, with final plans drawn up late in the decade. Actual construction began in 1991. The 6-lane highway would be replaced by an 8-to-10-lane underground expressway built directly beneath it. A brand-new 14-lane bridge would be built to cross over the Charles River, and the current Interstate 90—known as the Massachusetts Turnpike—would be extended.

Whereas the Hoover Dam was built in the middle of nothing but sun and desert, the Big Dig took place in the heart of bustling Boston. The trick was to determine how to progress with construction without disrupting the city's daily functions. The job resulted in the excavation of 16 million cubic yards (12.16 million cubic meters) of dirt—enough to fill a large sports stadium 15 times! It took 541,000 truckloads and 4,400 barge loads to move this material.

Although this construction project was not a dam, it had several things in common with the Hoover project. At the peak of its construction, the Big Dig employed 5,000 workers—approximately the same number that worked at Hoover Dam's peak. Cofferdams were part of the Hoover Dam construction, and a cofferdam played an important role in the Big Dig. To place the South Boston connection that runs from the underwater part of the Ted Williams Tunnel to the land-based approach, workers needed to create the widest, deepest circular cofferdam ever seen in North America. Hoover had its diversion tunnels, and the Big Dig had its own distinctive tunnels: Of the 161 miles (259.1 kilometers) of highway built during the project, half were tunnels. Both projects required an enormous amount of concrete—the Boston project placed 3.8 million cubic yards (2.888 million cubic meters) of the material. The amount of steel needed for reinforcement at the Big Dig was huge as well: the amount of steel used could create a 1-inch (2.5-centimeter) bar that could wrap itself around the globe at the equator! There was, however, one big *difference* between the two projects. The Hoover Dam had just one construction contract with Six Companies, but the Big Dig had a total of 118 separate construction contracts.

Completion of the Big Dig was official in 2007. The Central Artery would now be able to handle 245,000 vehicles a day, and the Ted Williams Tunnel would accommodate an additional 98,000 users daily. Instead of 10 straight hours of stop-and-go traffic, Boston commuters can expect more normal urban rush-hour traffic—with speeds of 30 mph (48.3 kph) slowing things down for just a few hours in the morning and evening.

(continued from page 45)

and individual name. The men who pioneered this project knew it by this name." In his memoirs, Hoover said he was not bothered in the least by this development. However, President Hoover's last-minute trip to the dam's construction site—just after he lost his bid for a second term in office—revealed his continuing passion for the project. The Bureau of Reclamation's Web site reports that, after Hoover ordered a brief stop while flying from Washington to California in November 1932, he spoke emotionally at the site:

> The waters of this great river, instead of being wasted in the sea, will now be brought into use by man. Civilization advances with the practical application of knowledge in such structures as the one being built here in the pathway of one of the great rivers of the continent. The spread of its values in human happiness is beyond computation.

The Return of Hoover Dam

More than 10 years later, on March 4, 1947, House Resolution 140 was introduced and later passed in Congress. The first paragraph states:

> Herbert Hoover, while Secretary of Commerce in 1922, presided as the representative of the Federal Government over two score meetings of the representatives of Arizona, California, Colorado, Nevada, New Mexico, Utah, and Wyoming for the formulation of the Colorado River Compact. He had a major part in bringing the States into agreement. This compact, signed November 24, 1922, made construction of the dam possible by allocating the waters of the river system between the upper and lower Colorado River Basin, settling a 25-year-old controversy. The Boulder Canyon Project Act, enacted December 21, 1928, when Mr. Hoover was President-elect, ratified the compact and authorized construction of a dam in Black Canyon or Boulder

Canyon, leaving to the Secretary of the Interior the choice of sites. It also laid upon him and the Secretary of the Interior extraordinary responsibilities.

The resolution further explains Hoover's involvement in the project and concludes with, "It is particularly timely that this measure honoring Mr. Hoover should come to the floor of the House at a time when he is completing the second of his great humanitarian missions for President Truman in the relief of world-wide suffering." The resolution and the name Hoover Dam became official one month later, when President Truman signed the document on April 30, 1947.

THE BIRTH OF SIX COMPANIES

The Boulder Dam was set to be the largest public works project the U.S. government had ever undertaken. The federal government accepted bids from hundreds of eager construction and engineering companies that hoped to walk away with a multimillion-dollar contract for a highly visible project. One of the government's requirements of the bidding companies was a $5 million ($60 million today) performance bond from whoever won the contract. Such a large amount of money became a deterrent for many potential bidders; it was too big a risk for most individual companies to take.

Contemplating a way to lessen this risk was Harry Morrison of the construction firm Morrison-Knudsen in Boise, Idaho. Morrison decided that the best way to bid for this coveted job was to form one company from several different ones. He already had an alliance with a company called Utah Construction and believed that it should be involved in what at the time was still being called the Black Canyon Project. Another choice of Morrison's was a highly regarded tunnel and sewer builder named Charlie Shea, who contributed $500,000 ($6 million today) toward the $5 million performance bond. Shea was known to be a real character and had the charm and connections needed to bring in other players. Among them were the Pacific Bridge Company and Felix Kahn from the San Francisco company that bore his name, MacDonald & Kahn.

Another longtime San Francisco contractor, Warren A. Bechtel, also wanted to be a part of Morrison's expanding team. Bechtel was the mentor to a much younger Oakland, California, resident named Harry Kaiser. Kaiser began work at the age of 11 after he had dropped out of school. Bechtel appreciated the younger man's ambition and work ethic as a road builder, so he suggested that the two of them ally themselves with the group Morrison was working to put together. This team of men and their companies called itself Six Companies—a name provided by Felix Kahn. It became an official corporation on February 19, 1931.

Six Companies now had the money available for the performance bond; the next step was to submit its bid. Bid submission was a tricky business. Rumor had spread that the Reclamation Services' engineers had already established precisely what the massive project should cost, so it was important that a bid not be too high yet remain profitable for the company submitting it. At Morrison's request, the men of Six Companies turned to Frank Crowe—one of the construction industry's most admired men and a valued employee of Morrison-Knudsen. Crowe made his calculations carefully and gave his recommended bid: $48,890,995 ($571.3 million today). This bid was more than appropriate; it was right on target. On March 4, 1931, when the sealed bids were opened at the reclamation office, Crowe's recommendation secured the government contract—the largest that had ever been awarded. Six Companies' winning bid was only $24,000 away from the Reclamation Services' own estimate.

CHAPTER 4

The People Who Built Hoover Dam

Once the legislation and funding for the Hoover Dam were approved, an army of workers was needed—5,000 at the construction's peak—to build what would come to be known as one of the seven wonders of the modern world. From the supervisors who led these men and created the dam's design to the workers themselves, everyone had an important contribution to make.

THE DAM'S WORKERS

The Hoover Dam's construction occurred at a desperate time in U.S. history. The stock market had crashed, leaving the Great Depression to settle in, and an almost unimaginable number of people were unemployed. Once the government approved the dam's creation, people realized that many hands would be needed to bring the ambitious project to fruition. As rumors started to circulate about potential jobs—even though Six Companies was not officially hiring yet—thousands of people packed up their families and moved to the harsh Nevada desert in search of work. In the film *American Experience: Hoover Dam*, worker

W.A. Davis said, "We was in a depression, flat on its back, belly up. The press made an announcement that the government was going to build the largest dam in the world, so I went over to a car lot and bought a '26 Essex car for $75 [$876 today], got into it and took off for Las Vegas."

Living in Ragtown

Families had two choices once they arrived in Nevada. They could find a place to settle in the tiny railroad town of Las Vegas—which had a population of 5,000—or they could simply make do in the undeveloped Black Canyon area. Most chose the latter option, believing that close proximity to the construction site would help in securing a job, because Las Vegas (at 30

BUILDING AMERICA NOW

HICKORY LOG CREEK

The city of Canton, Georgia, decided to build a dam and reservoir on Hickory Log Creek. The dam and its reservoir will provide a much-needed long-term source of drinking water—enough to keep residents from being thirsty until at least the year 2050. The reservoir also will serve as a backup water supply in case of drought. The dam is one of the state's largest not built by the Corps of Engineers or Georgia Power. Instead, the City of Canton joined forces with the Cobb County-Marietta Water Authority to accomplish what neither group could do alone.

Plans were developed in 2005 and the new dam—located just north of the city's downtown area—was completed in December 2007. It spans the river at a width of 950 feet (289.6 meters) and reaches toward the sky at a height of 180 feet (54.9 meters). The all-important reservoir will cover 370 acres (148 hectares) of land and provide residents with 15 miles (24.1 kilometers) of scenic shoreline.

miles, or 48.3 kilometers, away) would mean a tough commute. The floor of the Black Canyon became an impromptu town, covered with tents and cardboard boxes. Ragtown, as it was called, had its fair share of "campers" as well—cars with strategically placed cardboard and canvas that allowed people to live out of their vehicles. On the PBS *American Experience* Web site, one dam worker's daughter, Ila Clements-Davey, said of Ragtown, "There was just nothing. There was no facility. Nothing. There was nothing green around here. Everything was baked, hot, and brown."

Indeed, the area's temperatures, which regularly skyrocketed to 120°F (49°C), made Ragtown life difficult. One mother, Erma Godbey, draped wet sheets over her baby to keep the baby

The budget for the entire project ranged from $30 to $40 million. In addition to the dam and reservoir, the project includes an intake and pump station as well as a pipeline that will take water from the reservoir to the Etowah River—the city's current water supply.

One of the interesting aspects of this project is how the reservoir is filled. The total time estimated to fill the new lake is one to two years. The rate at which the reservoir fills is based on the dam's height and the guidelines set forth by the Georgia Safe Dams Program. The first third of the lake will fill at an uncontrolled rate, but for safety reasons, the next two phases of the filling process will be controlled. The second third of the reservoir will be filled at a rate of 2 feet (0.6 meters) per week. The final third of the filling will take place at a rate of 1 foot (0.3 meters) per week. When filled to capacity, the reservoir will hold 5 billion gallons (19 billion liters) of needed water, 44 million gallons (167.2 million liters) of which can be used each day by the city and county's people.

cool. This was the key to successful living in Black Canyon—improvisation. When a baby's diapers needed to be cleaned, a mother could boil them in bleach over a campfire. If a family needed a place to sit, a bench was formed by placing an ironing board on top of a couple crates.

Because the canyon's location was near the Colorado River, there was more than enough water for washing. Drinking the river's water, however, was another story; it tended to cause illnesses such as dysentery. Fresh milk and other food products that could spoil also were not an option. They could not be kept because of the intense heat. Therefore, meals in Ragtown often consisted of some type of canned food.

FRANK CROWE

In the 1930s, if you needed a dam built, Frank Crowe was the man to do it. Over the years, he had built up a remarkable reputation for efficiency and innovation in large-scale construction projects. Crowe was born in the town of Trenholmville in Quebec, Canada, in 1882. He moved to New England early in his life and studied civil engineering at the University of Maine in 1901. There, during the speech given by a member of the U.S. Reclamation Service, Crowe's keen interest in the western United States was sparked. By the end of the guest speaker's talk, Crowe had signed up for a summer job as a surveyor in the drainage basin of the Yellowstone River in Montana. This would be the start of his 20-year history with the Reclamation Service.

By 1924, Crowe was the acting general superintendent of construction for reclamation and was responsible for projects in 17 western states. He had become well known for developing efficient construction methods. In addition, the devoted engineer was instrumental in bringing new and unique construction equipment into use. One such innovation was the overhead cable system first used during the building of Idaho's Arrowrock Dam in 1911. This cable system would prove invaluable years

When the Hoover Dam project was announced in the middle of the Great Depression, thousands of people traveled to the area in hopes of finding employment. While some workers and their families settled in Las Vegas, Nevada, many others constructed makeshift homes in nearby Black Canyon *(above)*, which created a new community known as Ragtown.

later, during the Hoover Dam's construction. Another of Crowe's developments was the use of a pipe grid to transport cement pneumatically, or by using compressed air.

When the federal government began using private companies for dam projects, Crowe was not pleased; after two decades as a government worker with the Reclamation Service, he left to pursue work in the private sector. He joined Morrison-Knudsen, a company that had just aligned itself with Utah Construction for

HOOVER DAM'S MASCOT MUTT

The hardworking men of the Hoover Dam had a faithful companion at the site: A black-haired dog with a furry white chest often kept them company. No one really knows where the canine came from, but the men liked to say that he was born under the floorboards of one of their dormitories. The kitchen staff at Anderson Mess Hall even made a sack lunch each day for the furry worker, who traveled to and from the site with the men.

Sadly, the men's beloved coworker died "on the job." He was sleeping peacefully under a truck and out of the hot sun when he was crushed by the truck's tires because the driver did not know the dog was there. The dog was buried at the dam site, and his friends placed a memorial there in his honor.

the purpose of building dams together. This move allowed Crowe to do the work he loved—instead of being stuck in an office, he could get out into the field. During his time with Morrison-Knudsen, he supervised the construction of several dam projects, including Guernsey in Wyoming, Coombe in California, and Deadwood in Idaho. His next accomplishment, and the most recognized in the world of dam building, was the Hoover Dam.

Standing about 6 feet 4 inches (1.9 meters) in height, Crowe had a commanding presence as well as a reputation for being firm. Yet the long-time engineer also was viewed as a fair man who was good at his work. Among his achievements was taking a ragtag bunch of unemployed men and turning them into world-class builders.

CONDITIONS ON THE JOB

Once initial work began in the Arizona and Nevada deserts, conditions proved harsh. Summer temperatures often soared to 120°F

(48.9°), and winter temperatures could plummet to the freezing point and below. Regardless of the temperature, the men had to keep a quick pace—supervisors and managers had strict deadlines to enforce. The combination of working hard and fast in the scorching desert sun took its toll; a total of 14 men died of heat exhaustion. Helen Holmes's husband, Neil, collapsed from the

Dedicated to hard work and efficiency, Frank Crowe (above) was chosen to manage the construction of the Hoover Dam. Known for his hands-on style in managing other successful dam projects, Crowe stuck to his motto, "never my belly to a desk," and could be seen surveying the Hoover Dam work site at 2:00 A.M.

heat in the summer of 1931. In Dunar and McBride's book *Building Hoover Dam*, Holmes described the situation that summer:

> The men were going out with the heat. They called it passing out. Summer temperatures went terrifically high. The ambulance would go up so many times with the people . . . they'd have to pack them in ice and take them up. Of course, that siren—oh, it scared you 'cause you wondered if it might be your husband.

Extreme heat and cold and the pressure of deadlines were not the only hardships Hoover's workers faced. Six Companies sometimes skimped when it came to workers' safety. Because of the Depression, Six Companies knew that workers would be reluctant to complain—for every one man who worked on the site, there were hundreds more, possibly thousands, willing to take his place. The company sometimes chose to save a few pennies here and there, even if it meant endangering the workers' health and safety. Workers faced danger on the job every day: If they were not careful, they could suffer carbon monoxide poisoning, dehydration, or electrocution.

The Workers' Strike

The workers' fear of making demands changed in the summer of 1931. On August 7, Six Companies made the decision to reassign several men who were to work on the dam's diversion tunnels. The new assignment for this handful of workers would mean lower wages for them. Apparently, this was the last straw for the men at the site. The entire group of dam workers went on strike within only a few hours of Six Companies' demotion of a few of their brothers. Six Companies, trying to maintain calm and keep the situation at bay, explained that only 30 men would be affected by the reassignment. Yet Six Companies' words did little good. The workers took the opportunity to protest not only issues of pay but also the need for improved working conditions, such as readily available clean water and flush toilets, ice water at the site for drinking, and the use of Nevada and Arizona mining laws to establish safer working conditions.

Six Companies stood firm. Its leaders knew that the workers had little leverage, because they could so easily be replaced. Even Frank Crowe took the side of his employer, supporting the company rather than his men. He demanded that his workers return to their jobs or leave the dam site altogether. Crowe's stance on the labor dispute caused a division among the striking men.

Before giving up the battle, the workers turned to U.S. Secretary of Labor William Doak for help. Unfortunately for the men, Doak refused to become involved. Six Companies fired a good number of the striking workers. Afraid for their own jobs, the other men decided that any work was better than no work, and after eight days off the job everyone returned to the site.

Conditions Improve

The strike was not a complete failure, however: Six Companies effected a number of improvements afterward. The company promised that the pay cut the 30 men received would be the last any of the workers would ever have to worry about. Lighting was added to improve visibility at the site; water was made available for the workers; and the completion of Boulder City—the town that would take workers out of the misery of Ragtown—was made a higher priority. In Dunar and McBride's book, Elton Garrett, a Las Vegas journalist during the dam's construction, said of the strike:

> To a certain extent it did help. Management tried to be reasonable, and at times they improved conditions for the workers. They didn't give in to them and say, 'You can have all your wishes.' They didn't do that. The depression gave this whole country a climate where management could dictate terms pretty much.

BOULDER CITY

The government and Six Companies had not planned on Rag-town. Included in Six Companies' government contract was an agreement that the company would provide housing for 80 percent of its workers. Plans were to build a small, simple, bare-bones town. Walker Young had chosen a location 7 miles (11.2 kilometers) from the construction site to build a camp that thousands of people could call home. This camp—Boulder City—was intended to be ready for the workers before they arrived. However, the stock market crash and the Great Depression that followed spoiled that plan; anxious men hoping for any type of work arrived before even one house could be built. As soon as the funds to build Boulder City became available, work started on the tiny town.

Although Boulder City was for the workers hired by Six Companies, it was not run by the organization. Instead, Boulder City was considered a federal reservation; it fell under the jurisdiction of the Reclamation Service and the federal government. The "town" consisted of large dorms for single men and compact houses with one to three rooms for workers with wives and children.

A Plain Ol' Town

Construction in the town was ongoing, and workers built as many as three houses each day. The homes all looked alike; stories abound of men coming off their shift, returning home, and walking into the wrong house. In Dunar and McBride's *Building Hoover Dam*, Boulder City resident Wilma Cooper recalls what the quickly built homes were like: "These houses were put up in one day, child. You think you can put a house up in one day and have it look like anything? They never were comfortable, because there was no insulation in 'em. And the sheetrock inside was so thin—you sneeze on it, you'd blow a hole in it."

Besides roofs over the heads of workers and their families, Boulder City had little to offer. It had a library and a church, but

Boulder City *(above)* was constructed so that dam workers and their families could live in decent housing, rather that in the shacks that filled Ragtown. The community expanded rapidly, and soon 12 tons of fruit and vegetables, 5 tons of meat, and over 2 tons of eggs were being shipped to Boulder City's giant dining hall every week.

no school for the children. The government had not provided funds for a school, so the residents took it upon themselves to start one. Six Companies later helped to build a makeshift school where the town's children could receive some sort of education. A hospital—also paid for by Six Companies—opened in 1932, but its doctors and nurses tended only to the workers. No health care was provided for the women and children in Boulder City. One further addition to the town came during the workers' strike in 1931, when a security gate was placed at the entrance.

Sims Ely: Lawman

Sixty-nine-year-old Sims Ely was appointed Boulder City's mayor, judge, unofficial lawman, and conscience. Ely had been a newspaper editor in his younger days, as well as an employee of the justice department. The gruff Ely made certain that the town's residents followed the rules of no gambling and no drinking, which set Boulder City apart from nearby Las Vegas, known to cater to those particular vices. One Boulder City resident, Mary Ann Merrill, said about Ely on the PBS *American Experience* Web site, "I guess he was fair in a lot of ways, but he had his own ideas and he put them into practice. And you had to go by his rules. He thought of it as his town."

Three Square Meals a Day

One of the great benefits of living in Boulder City during the surrounding country's Depression was the mess hall run by Anderson Brothers, a California company. For an affordable $1.50 a day ($19.22 today), a resident of the town could get three daily meals—and eat as much at each meal as he or she desired. People in Boulder City ate better than most people in the United States at the time. Every day, the mess hall staff dished out 6,000 meals—or 12 tons (1.1 metric tons) of fruits and vegetables, 5 tons (0.5 metric tons) of meat, and 2.5 tons (0.2 metric tons) of eggs every week! Holiday meals were especially appreciated by the workers and their families. The University of Las Vegas Libraries Web site on the Hoover Dam quotes worker Marion Allen as saying, "You'd go up there [the mess hall], and Thanksgiving cost a whole 75 cents [$9 today]. The wife and I, 75 cents apiece; for the girl, it was free. So that cost $1.50 [$18 today]. You'd have turkey, roast beef, anything under the sun as long as you wanted."

A Temporary Town That Lasts

Unlike construction camps built for other projects, Boulder City did not disappear after the dam's completion. In fact, the town remained a federal reservation until 1959. By 1997, it had grown into a town with a population of 14,000.

AFRICAN AMERICANS ON THE JOB

In May 1931, the Colored Citizens Labor and Protective Association of Las Vegas raised a complaint against Six Companies and its hiring practices. The issue? Of the first 1,000 workers hired, none were African American. About a year later, Six Companies tried to explain its lack of black workers at the Hoover site. When National Association for the Advancement of Colored People (NAACP) field secretary William Pickens visited the area, Six Companies executives told him that they had experienced

A MATTER OF WAGES

What a man earned at the Hoover Dam work site depended on the specific job he was assigned to do. One truck driver, Lee Tilman, remembered working for 10 months straight—seven days each week—without one day off. Earning $5.00 a day ($60.00 today) for his efforts, he thought the pay was pretty good. On average, workers at the dam earned 62.5 cents per hour ($7.50 today), with the lowest earners receiving 50 cents per hour ($6.00 today) and the highest earners receiving $1.25 per hour ($15.00 today). Following are some examples of different workers' hourly wages: muckers and general laborers, 50 cents; jackhammer men and cement finishers, 62.5 cents; truck drivers, 50 to 75 cents; carpenters, 62.5 to 75 cents; tool sharpeners, crane operators, and electricians, 75 cents ($9.00 today); and shovel operators, $1.25.

Workers received only half of their wages in U.S. currency. The other half was paid in scrip—money printed by Six Companies that could only be spent in the Six Companies store in Boulder City. Workers could spend scrip on anything from food to new clothes.

problems with racial tension at other job sites. They cited as an example one nearly violent incident in which a Mexican foreman had been put in charge of a white crew.

Pressure to hire African-American workers continued to mount. Eventually, Six Companies president William Bechtel said they would add black workers to the current group of men—but this claim did not amount to much. By 1933, only 24 African-American men were employed at the Hoover Dam. Not only did African-American workers make up less than one per-cent of the Six Companies workforce, they also were forced to take the sweatiest and most undesirable job at the construction site—shoveling in the hot sun of the Arizona gravel pits.

These 24 workers faced segregation as well. African Ameri-cans (as well as Native Americans and Hispanics) were not allowed to live in Boulder City. This meant they rode segregated buses 30 miles (48.3 kilometers) to work from their homes in the slums of Las Vegas. As if that were not insult enough, at the job site the men were forced to drink from separate water buckets than those used by the thousands of white workers.

GORDON B. KAUFMANN

Gordon Kaufmann was a well-known architect famous for his modern designs. Originally from England, Kaufmann moved to southern California in 1913. He was chosen for the Hoover Dam project because people thought he could give the dam the strong, super-technology look they hoped it would have.

Kaufmann sat down with the plans originally drawn up by engineers from the Bureau of Reclamation. Their design had a distinctively classic style, but that style seemed to clash with the rest of the dam's smooth, clean design. Once Kaufmann reviewed these ideas, he set them aside and began work on his own sketches and ideas. The result was a fluid design meant to work seamlessly within the entire dam structure. The design was intended to showcase the dam's most impressive and significant feature—its gigantic concrete downstream face. As part of his design facelift, Kaufmann redesigned Hoover's power plant, giving it such touches as art deco metal fins for its windows. For the power plant's interior, he hired Alan True, who gave it its uniquely patterned floors and modern color schemes. In his design renovations, Kaufmann even took the dam's spillways into account, making sure that they would reflect the smooth, curved surfaces of the dam itself.

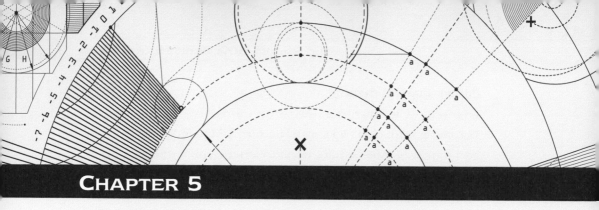

CHAPTER 5

Construction Begins

The Hoover Dam was an ambitious project: The massive, curved gravity dam would be the single-biggest construction project the United States had ever seen. Yet, another factor made building the dam an even more ambitious feat to accomplish—it was being built in the middle of nowhere, an area with no existing roads or sources of electricity. The previously untouched land meant that construction of an infrastructure would be needed *before* the construction of the dam.

DIVERTING THE COLORADO RIVER

Before work could begin on the massive dam, the mighty Colorado had to be dealt with. A dry, empty workspace was necessary to build the 726-foot-high (221.3-meter-high) dam. Workers would have to divert the Colorado's natural flow around the future work site. To accomplish this task, massive diversion tunnels and cofferdams were constructed.

Diversion Tunnels

To reroute the river, four diversion tunnels—each 56 feet (17.1 meters) in diameter and three-quarters of a mile (1.2 kilometers) long—were planned. These would be created by blasting right into the canyon's thick rock walls. Two tunnels would be constructed on the Nevada side, and another two would be constructed on the Arizona side. Work on the Nevada diversion tunnels began on May 12, 1931, with work on the Arizona tunnels starting not long afterward. Six Companies and its workers had a strict government deadline to meet. If the Colorado was not diverted within two and a half years, Six Companies would have to pay a hefty fine for each additional day it took to finish the job. The digging, blasting, and debris removal continued for 13 months, with men working 3 shifts 24 hours a day, 7 days a week.

Because no roads led into the canyon, men (as well as equipment) arrived at the work site by boat. Workers used 500 pneumatic drills, hoses, and compressors to make holes in the canyon rock where explosives could be placed. One of Frank Crowe's famous innovations was put to good use during this part of the process: Men were able to drill holes simultaneously by using "drilling jumbos." These 10-ton (9.1-metric ton) trucks were modified with three "stories" of planks that allowed 24 to 30 men to drill holes at once at three different heights. A total of eight drilling jumbos were used at the site and helped to quicken the pace.

Once holes were drilled, workers used dynamite to blast into the rock and break it into smaller pieces that could be hauled away by dump trucks. A ton (.9 metric tons) of dynamite was required for every 14 feet (4.3 meters) of tunnel that workers dug into the canyon wall. Before hauling could begin, however, expert miners checked the tunnels after blasting was complete to ensure that each newly dug tunnel was safe for other workers to enter. Worker Steve Chubbs described—in Dunar and McBride's *Building Hoover Dam*—what happened next: "They'd

In order to build the Hoover Dam in such a remote location, equipment and men had to be transported by boat from the Colorado River into Black Canyon. Rail lines and roads were eventually built, and the river waters were diverted to allow for large-scale construction. *Above*, the upstream view of the Hoover Dam before completion.

bring shovels and the trucks in. They called it muck. Ever hear the word? It was mostly broken rock. But it was an old word they picked up someplace. So they used to refer to the hauling out of the rock as mucking—mucking out. They'd muck out the rock and haul it away." Muckers cleared out the pieces of rock using power shovels and hand tools. Conveyor belts helped speed up the pace as well by removing rock from the area more quickly. The rock, once loaded onto dump trucks, was brought to the river's side canyons and dumped into piles. This rock was called spoil.

A MYSTERIOUS ILLNESS STRIKES

Working on the all-important diversion tunnels was a difficult job, but fall-ing rock was not the only danger the men faced. Workers drove diesel trucks into the tunnels as they progressed to haul out the newly blasted rock. Meanwhile, fellow workers breathed in the tunnel air while they com-pleted their own jobs. Inside the tunnels, fans and pipes circulated the air, but diesel exhaust remained. In the book *Building Hoover Dam*, worker John Gieck described his experience in the tunnels: "On the first of April 1932, I was sent down to the dam to do carpentry, building forms for the concrete in the [diversion] tunnels. Trucks and tractors working in there, carbon monoxide. I went to work down there one night, and there was 17 men in [my] crew. The next morning myself and 3 others was all that [was] left—all the rest was taken out sick." A number of workers eventually came down with what company doctors diagnosed as an unusual pneumo-nia. A few men even died. Workers at the site remained skeptical, however. They believed that tunnel fumes, not pneumonia, had affected the men.

Six men filed suit against Six Companies because of their illnesses. They had worked in the diversion tunnels and believed that their symp-toms were from carbon monoxide poisoning and may be permanent. Each worker demanded $75,000 ($1 million today) plus lost wages. Six Companies refused to budge and, instead of settling out of court, hired a private investigator. The investigator provided background information that made each worker look bad when his case went to court. Much like the attention some trials receive in the media today, the well-publicized carbon monoxide poisoning cases provided the people of Las Vegas with hours of entertainment.

As time wore on, more and more men came forward with symptoms. Although the suspected hazardous fumes were never proven to be the cause of the workers' sickness, Six Companies finally settled out of court for an undisclosed amount of money. Yet it may have been better if they had settled when the cases first arose—instead of settling with only 6 men, in the end the company had to settle with a total of 50 plaintiffs.

Lining the Tunnels

Frank Crowe was given the nickname "Hurry-Up" Crowe, and for good reason: He was consumed with deadlines. Thanks to Crowe's innovations and inspiration, and his hardworking team of men, the diversion tunnels were dug out in only 14 months—several months ahead of schedule. Digging out was just the first step, however. Before the tunnels would be complete and ready to use, they had to be lined with a layer of concrete. A concrete mixing plant was built three-quarters of a mile (1.2 kilometers) from the construction site specifically for this purpose. Its first batch of concrete was produced on March 3, 1932. The plant provided the concrete needed for both the tunnel lining and the dam's lower levels.

The concrete tunnel lining was created in three stages. The first stage involved pouring the base, or invert, to place the concrete. To accomplish this task, workers used gantry cranes that ran on rails throughout the entire length of each tunnel. The second stage was pouring the sidewalls, which was done by using moveable sections of steel form. The last stage was filling in the overheads, which workers accomplished using pneumatic guns. When it was finished, the concrete lining was 3 feet (0.9 meters) thick, shrinking each tunnel's original diameter of 56 feet (17.1 meters) to 50 feet (15.2 meters).

On November 14, 1932, the new tunnels were put to the test when water flowed through them for the first time. The tunnels were capable of carrying more than 1.5 million gallons (5.7 million liters) of water each second, but this was only the first step. There was much work to be done, including the construction of a powerhouse, intake tunnels, and the enormous dam itself.

Cofferdams

To keep the dam's work site isolated and protected from possible flooding, two temporary dams, or cofferdams, were among the project's many construction plans. Workers made the cofferdams by using 100 trucks to dump dirt, rock, and debris into the water

By sliding sticks of dynamite into holes bored into the canyon wall, workers were able to blast and excavate large diversion tunnels. These tunnels, each about the size of a 4-lane highway, were lined with 3 feet of concrete, allowing river water to be transported away from the construction site at a rate of 1.5 million gallons per second. *Above*, workers inside one of the diversion tunnels in Black Canyon.

at a rate of one truckload every 15 seconds. This frenzied pace of dredging and dumping went on for five months.

The design of the upper cofferdam was such that, if water shot through the diversion tunnels at a speed of 200,000 cubic feet (6,000 cubic meters) per second, the water would still be 13 feet (4 meters) below the cofferdam's crest—thus protecting the work site from any flooding. Engineers used the 200,000-cubic-feet-per-second benchmark because that was the largest flow ever recorded at Black Canyon.

Although the Colorado had not yet been diverted through the tunnels, workers started on the cofferdams in September 1932. The upper cofferdam was to be located 600 feet (182.9 meters) downriver, at the site of the diversion tunnels' inlets. Again, as with construction of the dam itself, building of the first cofferdam could not begin without the completion of some preparatory work. In this case, workers had to remove 250,000 cubic yards (190,000 cubic meters) of silt. When the upper cofferdam was complete, it stood 98 feet (29.9 meters) high—30 feet (9.1 meters) beyond the top of the diversion tunnels. Its base was 750 feet (228.6 meters) thick.

Work on the lower cofferdam was delayed until the high scaling work at the site of the future power plant and outlet works was complete. When this second temporary dam was finished, it stood 66 feet (20.1 meters) tall, stretched 350 feet (106.7 meters) across, and had a base 550 feet (167.6 meters) thick. Including the rock fill layer that covered the cofferdam's downstream side, 230,000 cubic yards (174,800 cubic meters) of earth and an additional 63,000 cubic yards (47,880 cubic meters) of rock had been used in the dam's creation.

Once the cofferdams were ready, the water that rested between them was pumped out. Then workers began to excavate the area, using steam shovels to remove 40 feet (12.2 meters) of rock, sand, and silt from the riverbed.

Because the cofferdams were made of a soft earth fill, some feared that these temporary dams might be damaged if a flood should occur. To further protect these cofferdams and the work site, a rock barrier 54 feet (16.5 meters) high, 375 feet (114.3 meters) long, and 200 feet (61 meters) wide at the base was created. It sat 350 feet (106.7 meters) downriver from the two cofferdams. Finally, the diversion tunnels, cofferdams, and rock barrier were complete. All of this work was put to the test in the spring of 1933. With the spring came floods, and everyone waited to see if the work would hold. Fortunately all of the hard work proved successful, and construction of the dam itself was ready to begin.

HIGH SCALERS

Perhaps one of the toughest and most dangerous jobs one could have during the years of the Hoover Dam's construction was that of high scaler. This job entailed the removal of loose rock from the canyon walls to ready them for the dam's construction by smoothing them over and shaping them. Men used 44-pound (20-kilogram) jackhammers and dynamite. The trick was to do this work while suspended by a rope that hung from the top of the canyon wall. High scalers sat in midair contraptions called bosun's chairs and had to have the heavy jackhammers lowered down to them. Then they would position the jackhammer in place by hand. Once the needed hole was drilled, the high scaler placed his dynamite and ignited a blast. Finally, the men used crowbars (if necessary) to free any loosened rock that clung to the canyon wall after the blast.

The job's danger came not only from hanging hundreds of feet in the air above ground but also from maneuvering among the air hoses and power lines that shared the airspace above the work site. Falling rocks and dropped tools posed regular threats to high scalers—in fact, falling rocks and other objects were the number-one cause of death among the men who worked on the Hoover Dam.

A special kind of person was needed to perform such a demanding and dangerous job. The men who worked as high scalers came from backgrounds as varied as sailors and circus acrobats, and some were Native American. A number of high scalers liked to show off when the bosses were not looking. They would swing out on their thin ropes and perform stunts for the men below. These high-profile workers even competed against one another, seeing who could swing out the farthest or highest or who could dream up the most impressive stunt.

Constant danger meant that life as a high scaler was not always fun and games. Louis Fagan, known as "The Human Pendulum," often completed unusual tasks as part of his high scaling job. A crew of men was needed to complete work past a particularly large boulder that jutted out from the canyon wall. Twice a day, over the course of several weeks, it was Fagan's job to transport each worker along a high wire—an act one might expect to see at a circus. The man to be transported would wrap his legs around Fagan's waist and hold tight to the rope. Then, in one giant leap, the two men would swing out and over the rocky obstacle. Fagan would then swing back and ready himself to take the next man over.

When Bureau of Reclamation engineer Burl R. Rutledge fell from atop the canyon ridge, high scalers were responsible for his daring rescue. Oliver Cowan was hard at work, high scaling 25 feet (7.6 meters) below the rim, when he heard Rutledge fall. Cowan's immediate reaction was to swing out, where he was able to grab hold of Rutledge by his leg. Fellow high scaler Arnold Parks joined in the rescue by swinging over and pinning Rutledge against the canyon wall. Cowan and Parks were able to hold the stunned engineer there until someone dropped another line that the men placed securely around him. Rutledge was then pulled back to safety.

THE CONCRETE OF HOOVER DAM

The Hoover Dam was indeed special. This dam alone required almost as much concrete for its construction as did all of the Bureau of Reclamation's previous dams combined. On June 6, 1933, building of the actual dam structure began when the first bucket of concrete was poured into the canyon bottom. Rumors abound that, of the numerous deaths that occurred during the dam's construction, one or more men were buried alive inside the dam's massive concrete. Yet, because of the way the concrete was poured—into individual interlocking blocks—this would have been nearly impossible.

The Pouring Process

The concrete used in the Hoover Dam could not be poured all at once. Had the dam been built this way, it would have taken 125 years to cool and harden completely. It would also have caused cracking within the concrete that would compromise the dam's integrity. Instead, the dam was built as a series of individual interlocking columns, with each column formed from a group of concrete blocks. These blocks varied in size—the smallest were approximately 25 x 25 feet (7.6 x 7.6 meters), the largest were about 25 x 60 feet (7.6 x 18.3 meters), and both averaged 5 feet (1.5 meters) in depth. The blocks were made by pouring either 4 or 8 cubic yards (3 or 6.1 cubic meters) of concrete into bottom dump buckets.

Frank Crowe's overhead cable system lifted the buckets from the ground, transported them, and then lowered them to their proper locations. Nine of these cable systems were used during the dam's construction. Five of them were attached to movable towers and could be used in various places. Once a bucket reached its destination and was poured into a dam form block, a team of five or six men called puddlers would stomp on the concrete to ensure that it contained no air holes. Large blocks increased in size only 2 to 3 inches (5.1 to 7.6 centimeters) at a time, and small blocks increased in height just 6 inches (15.2 centimeters) at a time. That meant that death by enveloping concrete was unlikely.

Hardening

One-inch (2.5-centimeter) steel piping helped to cool each concrete block. Workers placed these thin-walled pipes inside each form. For initial cooling, when the concrete was first poured, river water was used inside the pipes. When this round of cooling was complete, chilled water sent from a refrigeration plant at the lower cofferdam finished the job.

The pipes did more than just cool the hardening concrete. Once they were no longer needed for that task, workers used pneumatic guns to fill them with grout, making them an integral part of the dam's inner structure.

Grout was necessary in another area of the dam's completion as well. A potential problem with using individual blocks to build the dam was that hairline cracks might eventually develop between them. To combat this problem, the upstream and downstream sides of every block were created with grooves that ran vertically and interlocked. After the blocks cooled, grout was forced into these joints to make the dam even stronger.

While the Hoover Dam's vast amounts of concrete were being poured, inspectors and technicians from the Bureau of Reclamation watched over the process. They checked to make sure that the concrete cooled at the same rate. They looked for any movement in the giant structure as it went up, and they ensured that no fissures occurred in the concrete through which water might seep. In Dunar and McBride's book, worker Steve Chubbs talks about his role in the process:

> I think there were 8 or 10 of us. It was all mapped out for us. We worked in shifts measuring stress and strain, the temperature of the concrete. [We] put in strain meters and thermometers in the concrete according to the specifications. Then after they were in, we had to read them every eight hours for two or three weeks, so it kept us pretty busy.

The last bucket of concrete was poured on February 6, 1935—two years ahead of schedule and under budget. Its placement marked the end of construction on the dam itself. The Hoover Dam soared into the sky, reaching a final height of 726.5 feet (221.4 meters). It took a while longer to complete the final features of the dam. Six Companies had been given seven years to complete the entire construction; in an astonishing feat against time, the entire project was finished on March 1, 1936—two years ahead of schedule.

SPILLWAYS

The spillways located on each side of the dam were built to protect it from great flooding. These spillways keep water from going over the dam's top. Their function is much like that of an overflow hole of a bathtub: When bath water reaches a certain level, it gets sucked into the hole and sent down the drain.

To create room for these two spillways, workers had to excavate more than 600,000 cubic yards (456,000 cubic meters) of rock. These concrete-lined open channels were built 650 feet (198.1 meters) long, 150 feet (45.7 meters) wide, and 170 feet (51.8 meters) deep. Their concrete lining measured 18 inches (45.7 centimeters) thick on the wall sides and 24 inches (61 centimeters) thick on the

Hanging high above ground, workers called high scalers *(above)* were responsible for removing loose rock from the canyon walls. High scalers endured the most treacherous work in the dam's construction: Carrying tools and a large water bag, they used 44-pound jackhammers to drill dynamite holes into the canyon walls.

bottom. In creating the spillways, workers used a total of 127,000 cubic yards (96,520 cubic meters) of concrete.

The spillways were placed 27 feet (8.2 meters) below the dam's top; if any water rose that high, it would flow into the spillways and down the inclined tunnels connected to them. These tunnels measured 600 feet (182.9 meters) long and 50 feet (15.2 meters) in diameter, and they were built from the spillway toward the ground at a steep angle. There, they connected to two of the original diversion tunnels. The discharge from each spillway was controlled by a large drum gate at each spillway's crest. These gates could be controlled either automatically or manually. The maximum velocity of the water in the spillways was close to 175 feet per second (53.3 meters per second) or 120 miles per hour (193.1 kph). At its maximum, the water flow over each spillway would be nearly equal to the flow over Niagara Falls!

Since their completion, the spillways have been used only twice—once in August 1941 to test their function, and once during an unusually wet spring in 1983. That year, the spillways performed the job they were created to do. Water flowed into them at a rate of 52,000 cubic feet (1,560 cubic meters) per second, minimizing the flooding that occurred downstream.

HYDROELECTRICITY: THE BASICS

Hydroelectric power is a form of clean energy. It does not cause air pollution, create chemical leftovers, or produce toxic waste. To create this electrical energy, water must fall from above to an area below. The greater the distance the water falls, the more electrical energy can be produced. The fall of water can occur naturally, such as the movement of water in a waterfall or water traveling down the slope of a mountain. Although the natural fall of water *can* produce electrical energy, it is not necessarily the *best* way to produce it. Such sources, when they occur in nature, are not always reliable. When weather is dry and little rain falls, there may not be enough water to create the energy needed.

This is where dams come in. A dam can store water, guaranteeing that there will be enough to create energy on a regular basis. Using a dam, a plant can be built in a location that has no natural fall of water. The dam and plant work together to create the electrical energy. First, the dam holds back enough water to cause the water level to reach a high point, or head. Next, the water is released so that it falls with force; this is the force of gravity at work. Finally, this water hits the blades of water wheels below. These spinning turbines use mechanical energy to turn a power generator. The generator then takes the mechanical energy and turns it into electrical energy, or electricity.

Niagara Falls, New York, boasts the site of the first hydroelectric station ever built. Completed in November 1896, the plant provided electricity for the city of Buffalo, New York, 20 miles (32.2 kilometers) away. From that date in the late 1800s to the year 1977, hydroelectric power plants grew by leaps and bounds. In 1977, hydroelectric stations were responsible for producing almost one-third of all the electrical power in the world.

A Generator's Parts

A generator, like the 17 found in the Hoover plant, has five main parts. The first is called the *exciter*. The exciter is a much smaller generator that produces electricity sent to the *rotor*—one of the other main parts—and charges it magnetically. The rotor consists of a series of electromagnets known as *poles*, which are connected to another of the five major parts—the *shaft*. When the shaft rotates, the rotor does as well. The shaft connects both the exciter and the rotor to the turbine. The last major component of the generator is called the *stator*. This crucial piece is a nonmoving copper wire coil. Electricity is made when the rotor's magnets spin past the copper wiring of the stator.

THE HOOVER POWER PLANT

At the foot of the Hoover Dam is its own U-shaped power plant. The plant houses 17 generators that together produce more

THE HARD-BOILED HAT

The danger of debris falling from above led to another innovation in construction—the hard hat. The Hoover Dam construction site is believed to be the first place this protective gear was put into use. Workers, hoping to protect themselves from falling rock and other debris, cleverly took two caps and placed them one on top of the other, with the bills facing in opposite directions. They dipped these double-billed hats in tar, let them harden, and then repeated the process several more times. It did not take long for word to spread about how these makeshift hardhats had saved several men from what might have been deadly accidents. A few men were hit so hard by falling rocks that their jaws were broken; however, because they had their hard hats on, they did not receive skull fractures. Six Companies put in an order for these new hardhats and purchased them for every man on the job. The result was a marked reduction in the number of deaths that occurred.

than 4 billion kilowatt-hours each year—enough for 1.3 million people. (A kilowatt-hour is the unit of work or energy equivalent to that done by one kilowatt of power acting for one hour. One kilowatt equals 1,000 watts or 1.34 horsepower.)

The power plant has two wings, each of which measures 650 feet (198.1 meters) in length. Inside each of these wings are two station-service units powered by giant water wheels. Each station-service unit generates 2,400 kilowatts of electricity. This energy is used to help run the plant itself, powering its lights as well as the cranes, pumps, motors, compressors, and other electrical equipment necessary for both the dam and the plant.

Part of the original appeal of the Hoover Dam was that the energy it produced would eventually help pay for its initial cost. In 1940, the Boulder Canyon Project Act passed. Using this legislation, the secretary of the interior could decide what to charge for the energy created by the plant and determine how the money that was generated should be spent. By May 31, 1987, the goal was achieved: The energy produced and sold by this time paid for the project's original construction costs.

Southern California Edison and Los Angeles Water and Power were responsible for running the plant, under the supervision of the Bureau of Reclamation, until 1987—the year their 50-year electric service contracts expired. From that time forward, the Bureau of Reclamation took over the plant's operation and maintenance.

Over time, changes have been necessary at the plant site. In 1984, Congress passed the Hoover Power Plant Act. This act provided for upgrades to the 17 generators as well as the construction of additional visitor facilities and the Hoover Dam Bypass Bridge. As a result of this legislation, all 17 of the original generators were replaced between 1986 and 1993.

The Hoover Power Plant has been a great success. Between 1939 and 1949, it was the largest such plant in the United States. In recent years, however, its electricity-generating capacity has diminished due to continuing drought conditions and lower reservoir levels.

INTAKE TOWERS

While the dam's concrete was being poured, four significant structures were being built above the dam itself. These are the dam's intake towers. Each comprises 93,674 cubic yards (71,192 cubic meters) of concrete and 15.3 pounds (6.9 kilograms) of steel. Each structure is 82 feet (25 meters) wide at the base, a little over 63 feet (19.2 meters) in diameter at the top, and between 29 and 30 feet (8.8 and 9.1 meters) in interior diameter. Each of these four units is responsible for supplying one-fourth of the water the turbines need to create electricity.

The four intake towers—two on the Arizona side and two on the Nevada side—control the amount of water flowing through them by two cylindrical gates. These gates are located near the middle and bottom of each tower and are protected by sturdy trash racks that weigh 7 million pounds (3.1 million kilograms) each.

PENSTOCKS

At the Hoover Dam, water reaches the turbines by way of four 30-foot (9.1-meter) diameter penstocks—two on each side of the river—that connect the intake towers to the power plant and outlet valves. An entire fabrication facility was needed at the dam site to create the penstocks. They were put together using sepa-

In order to deliver concrete to the work areas without exhausting his employees, Frank Crowe designed an elaborate cable system to transport materials throughout the work site. With this system, construction became faster and more efficient as buckets full of concrete reached workers every 78 seconds. *Above*, a crane lifts a load of concrete to workers on the canyon wall.

rate 11-foot (3.4-meter) sections that weighed 80 tons (72.6 metric tons) each. Two of these smaller sections were joined to make one 22-foot (6.7-meter) piece that was then moved to the canyon rim by tractor. Next, the largest of Frank Crowe's cableways carried this 160-ton (145.2–metric ton) section to the canyon base, where sections were joined together until they formed 1 mile (1.6 kilometers) of connected pipe.

Water is sent through the penstocks via special gates that control the amount that passes through. The minimum head, or vertical distance the water travels downward, is 420 feet (128 meters), and the maximum is 590 feet (179.8 meters). On average, the head is 510 to 530 feet (155.4 to 161.5 meters).

THE DIVERSION TUNNELS TRANSFORM

When the diversion tunnels were no longer needed to reroute the Colorado River around the dam site, they were partially filled with concrete and used for another purpose. The two inner tunnels were each filled up to one-third of their length below the inlets. The 30-foot (9.1-meter) diameter steel pipes would now connect the reservoir's intake towers to both the power plant's penstocks and the canyon wall outlet works. Located at the outlets of the two inner tunnels are 50-x-35-foot (15.2-x-10.7-meter) gates. Each gate can be closed whenever necessary—for example, when the tunnels need to be emptied for inspection or repair work.

The outer tunnels were filled for half of their length. The two open downstream halves now could be used as spillway outlets. Gigantic 50-x-50-foot (15.2-x-15.2-meter) steel bulkhead gates permanently shut the inlets of the two outer tunnels. Each gate weighed an unbelievable 3 million pounds (1.35 million kilograms) and had to be transported to the site by 42 railroad cars.

THE HOOVER DAM RESERVOIR

The water held back by the immense dam created the largest human-made reservoir in the world—Lake Mead—in one of the driest places on Earth. The only real way to test the dam was to fill its reservoir, a task that took six years.

Lake Mead spans 157,900 acres (63,160 hectares) or 247 square miles (642.2 square kilometers). It extends 110 miles (177 kilometers) upstream toward the Grand Canyon as well as 35 miles (56.3 kilometers) up the Virgin River. The width of the lake varies depending on its location. In the canyons, it can stretch anywhere from several hundred feet to 8 miles (12.9 kilometers). With a normal elevation of 1,221 feet (372.2 meters), the Hoover Dam's reservoir can hold 28.5 million acre-feet (3.4 million cubic meters) of water. (An acre-foot equals the amount of water needed to cover one acre, or 0.4 hectares, of area at a depth of one foot, or 0.3 meters.) One acre-foot equals about 326,000 gallons (1.2 million liters). The amount of water in Lake Mead could cover the entire state of Pennsylvania up to 1 foot (.3 meters).

THE DEDICATION OF THE HOOVER DAM

After the final concrete was poured, President Franklin D. Roosevelt came to the site on September 30, 1935 to speak at its dedication ceremony. Among his remarks, Roosevelt said,

> Ten years ago the place where we are gathered was an unpeopled, forbidding desert. In the bottom of a gloomy canyon, whose precipitous walls rose to a height of more than a thousand feet, flowed a turbulent, dangerous river. The mountains on either side of the canyon were difficult to access with neither road nor trail, and their rocks were protected by neither trees nor grass from the blazing heat of the sun. The site of Boulder City was a cactus-covered waste. The transformation wrought here in these years is a twentieth-century marvel.

He ended his speech with the words, "This is an engineering victory of the first order—another great achievement of

American resourcefulness, American skill and determination. That is why I have the right once more to congratulate you who have built Boulder Dam and on behalf of the Nation to say to you, 'Well done.'"

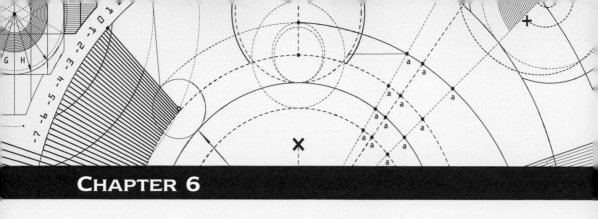

CHAPTER 6

Dams in the World Today

The Hoover Dam's construction was seen as progress in the 1930s and for several decades dam building continued at a good pace. With time, however, people began to realize that dams had drawbacks as well as benefits. In today's world, dam construction can be filled with controversy, and there are even movements to promote the tearing down of these human-made structures. But given the millions of people who travel to see it from around the world, there can certainly be no doubt that Hoover Dam has become, and will remain, an iconic feat of engineering.

THE DEBATE ON DAMS

A great deal of controversy currently surrounds the subject of dams. In fact, there are even disagreements about the number of new dams being constructed in the world today. Some environmental organizations claim that the number of new dams is decreasing. The Sierra Club says that dams in the modern world are "falling like dominoes in the name of river restoration." However, the United States Committee on Large Dams says that, if you look at the number of dams being built worldwide—rather than just in the United States—the 36,000 dams currently in use are ever increasing. As populations continue to grow, the committee claims, more dams will be necessary to keep up with the demand for water.

From the 1930s to the 1970s, dam construction was equated with modernization and economic progress. Dam building reached its peak in the 1970s, when it is estimated that around the world two or three large dams were in early planning stages each day. Over time, more information became available about how these dams affected the surrounding people and environment. Part of their impact includes an estimated displacement of anywhere from 40 to 80 million people worldwide.

Dams and their diversion of a river's natural flow have affected approximately 60 percent of the world's rivers. Dams have obvious benefits—providing drinking water, flood protection, and water for irrigation chief among them. Yet, dams—especially large ones—have drawbacks as well. Today, people debate whether dams are helpful or harmful.

Dam Benefits

Benefits of large dams go beyond flood control, irrigation, and the creation of recreational lakes. For example, dams can help with soil conservation. It is probably obvious that a flood can ruin crops. What may be less obvious is that a flood can actually destroy the land for future use by carrying away the rich topsoil needed to nourish and grow a crop. By preventing floods in the first place, dams ensure that soil will be protected.

In the United States today, there are more than 2,000 dams with hydropower plants at their base. A further benefit of large dams is the hydropower produced by these plants. Currently, this hydroelectric power is the most plentiful and efficient source of renewable energy—hydropower provides 90 percent of all renewable electrical energy in the nation. The energy produced at hydropower plants is much cleaner than the energy that comes

THE STORY OF *MISS VEGAS*

These days, the Hoover Dam hosts millions of curious visitors each year. But way back in the summer of 1930, a man named P. Leonard Lacey was the first to capitalize on the tourist trade that such a feat of engineering could bring. Lacey, the operator of a small boat service in the area, built the Boulder Dam Pier on the Colorado River. On this two-story boat landing, tourists could board boats and see the sights of Black Canyon. The first of Lacey's water vessels was an open, 33-foot (10.1-meter) boat that could seat 42 sightseers. Its name was *Miss Vegas*.

Miss Vegas did not have a very long run. For less than a year, she took couples on romantic moonlight cruises into the dark canyon and chartered government engineers and officials who needed to make last-minute inspections before the dam's construction began. Her excursions came to an end in the spring of 1931, when Lacey's giant pier had to be demolished to clear the way for a government railroad. Lacey sold *Miss Vegas* to none other than Six Companies, which used the boat to carry equipment and workers during the dam's construction.

from fossil fuels, which results in less air pollution. According to the United States Society on Dams, if all of today's hydropower energy were produced using coal, pollution from coal would increase 16 percent.

Dam Drawbacks

A major concern of environmental groups, such as the Sierra Club, is the possible extinction of plants and animals native to a dam's environment. The Sierra Club states that dams "devastate fish runs and destroy fragile ecosystems." Reservoirs, once filled, can cover entire forests, and areas where dams are built may also lose wetlands and farmlands as a result. In certain places, dams have caused the extinction of some fish and other aquatic creatures. In addition, birds may leave the vicinity when forests are no longer present.

Another drawback of constructing a new dam is that some-times people—even entire towns—need to be relocated to make way for the project. In March 1997, people from 20 countries including Argentina, Chile, China, India, Russia, Thailand, and the United States gathered in Curitiba, Brazil, for the First International Meeting of People Affected by Dams. On March 14, they made a declaration "affirming the right to life and livelihood of people affected by dams." The first few paragraphs of the declaration read as follows:

> We, the people from 20 countries gathered in Curitiba, Brazil, representing organizations of dam-affected people and of opponents of destructive dams, have shared our experiences of the losses we have suffered and the threats we face because of dams. Although our experiences reflect our diverse cultural, social, political and environmental realities, our struggles are one.
>
> Our struggles are one because everywhere dams force people from their homes, submerge fertile farmlands, forests and sacred places, destroy fisheries and supplies of clean water, and cause the social and cultural disintegration and economic impoverishment of our communities.
>
> Our struggles are one because everywhere there is a wide gulf between the economic and social benefits promised by dam builders and the reality of what has happened after dam construction. Dams have almost always cost more than was projected, even before including environmental and social costs. Dams have produced less electricity and irrigated less land than was promised. They have made floods even more destructive. Dams have benefited large landholders, agribusiness corporations and speculators. They have dispossessed small farmers; rural workers; fishers; tribal, indigenous and traditional communities.

The World Commission on Dams

In response to the increasing debate on dams—especially large ones—a commission of 12 members was established in February 1998. The World Commission on Dams had two main goals.

Holding back the waters of the newly formed Lake Mead, the Hoover Dam was unveiled to the public in 1935—earlier than expected and millions of dollars under budget. During the dam's dedication ceremony, President Franklin Delano Roosevelt surveyed the structure, and announced, "I came, I saw, I was conquered." *Above*, the dedication ceremony gave people a chance to admire the dam for the first time.

The first goal was to review the effectiveness of large dams and to suggest alternatives for the water resources and energy that such dams provide. The second objective was to develop guidelines and standards to be used globally in the planning, design, construction, operation, maintenance, and removal of dams.

In its report "Dams and Development: A New Framework for Decision-Making" released on November 16, 2000, the commission began by stating, "The global debate about large dams is at once overwhelmingly complex and fundamentally simple." It claimed that dams had made an important and significant contribution to society's progress, but the commission also acknowledged that this progress had come at a price—such as displaced communities, higher taxes, and interference with the natural environment.

TEARING DOWN DAMS

Although some countries, such as China, continue with the construction of large-scale dam projects, the commissioning of large dams in the United States has come to a standstill. In fact, pressure is mounting—mainly from environmental organizations—to tear down a number of large dams across the country. One of the first big dams to come down in the United States was North Carolina's Quaker Neck Dam, located on the Neuse River. The dam's teardown was an attempt to save fisheries and renew the river. Once Quaker Neck was dismantled, 75 miles (120.7 kilometers) of river and 90 miles (144.8 kilometers) of tributaries were reopened.

DAM FAILURES AND DISASTERS

Because of the potential destruction that dam failures can cause, they often receive a large amount of publicity. Yet the overall incidence of dam failures is low when the number of dams in existence is taken into consideration. Following are a few dam failures and disasters that made the papers—and history.

Vaiont, Italy

Tragedy struck the town of Vaiont, Italy, on October 9, 1963. That day, rock and earth moved down the mountainside when the weight of the Vaiont Dam's own reservoir water caused a landslide. The spillage into the reservoir in turn caused a great wave of water to rush over the dam wall into the valley below. It was a testament to the dam's strength and construction that, in a flood of water that killed more than 2,000 individuals and ruined several villages, the dam itself remained remarkably intact and was kept in use until 1977.

Teton Dam

In 1976, the Teton Dam—an earthfill embankment dam in Idaho—had just been built, and the dam's reservoir was filling

BUILDING AMERICA NOW

TEARING DOWN EDWARDS DAM

Amid the increasing debate over dams, some dams are being removed for a variety of reasons. The Edwards Dam in Augusta, Maine, concerned local residents. The hydropower it produced only provided 0.1% of the state's total power, and this small amount did not seem to outweigh the damage done to fish migration and passage.

Before the dam could be removed, a lot had to be considered. For example, before the project could be approved, officials had to know the answer to the following question: When the reservoir was lowered, would it cause the steep embankments to cave into the river? Such an event could result in devastating mudslides and peoples' homes falling into the river. To answer this and other questions, the Federal Energy Regulatory Commission hired several companies to investigate the river system, the environmental impact of the dam's removal, and the total cost of such a project.

with water. On June 5, someone spotted a hole in the dam's 300-foot (91.4-meter) wall, through which water was leaking. Because of this observer's keen eye, people were warned in advance of the dam's possible failure, and most people located below the dam moved to safety before it burst. The advance warning had come early enough that a television crew was able to set up and film the dam the moment it ruptured. The Teton Dam's failure resulted in the flooding of two cities—Sugar City and Reburg. Despite the early warning provided, 14 people were killed and the torrent of water and sand caused more than a billion dollars' worth of damage.

After thorough studies, approval was given for teardown of the Edwards Dam—an actual timber crib, which means that it is a log structure filled with rocks and capped with concrete. The removal took place in two stages in the summer of 1999. The first stage involved the building of a large cofferdam that stretched from the west shore to the dam itself. Once this cofferdam was in place, workers excavated 90 feet (27.4 meters) of the dam. After the excavation was finished, they breached—or made a gap in—the cofferdam, which allowed the reservoir to lower its level 8 feet (2.4 meters).

The second stage of the teardown involved the same process, this time using a smaller cofferdam on the dam's east side. Here, 300 feet (91.4 meters) of the dam was removed. The smaller cofferdam was then breached, and the reservoir lowered the rest of the way. The 17 miles (27.4 kilometers) of river now flow their natural course and will once again provide a home for endangered fish species such as short-nosed and Atlantic sturgeon, striped bass, shad, and alewife.

Other Failures

An earth dam in western India collapsed under pressure from floodwaters. The incident, which occurred in 1979, killed 5,000 people; numerous others lost their homes. Perhaps the worst disaster in the history of dams was a failure in Philadelphia, Pennsylvania, in 1889. When the dam burst, it not only crushed houses by the hundreds, it also killed a total of 10,000 people.

HOOVER DAM TODAY

The Hoover Dam is now run by the Lower Colorado Dams Office of the Bureau of Reclamation. In addition to managing, operating, and maintaining America's most famous dam, this Reclamation Office runs other dams on the Lower Colorado, such as the Davis and Parker dams.

Visiting Hoover Dam

Hoover Dam has been a popular tourist spot since its completion. Every year, nearly one million visitors come to the famous dam and participate in the Bureau of Reclamation's guided tour program. Visitors initially could take part in a hard hat tour that took place inside the power plant, but that tour has since been replaced by a primarily self-guided "Discovery Tour." With a ticket, visitors have access to the Visitor Center and a variety of dam exhibits. At several locations, staff members still provide informational talks. The Bureau of Reclamation estimates that a full tour of Hoover Dam, seeing everything there is to see, should take a visitor about two hours.

So, what can people do on their visit? Several displays—including murals, maps, and photos—provide a thorough introduction to the famous dam's history. Another exciting option is to take an elevator 500 feet (152.4 meters) down, right into the rock wall of Black Canyon. Once there, visitors walk through a 250-foot-long (76.2-meter-long) corridor that has been drilled out of the surrounding rock. At the end of this rock tunnel, tourists can take in the Nevada wing's 650-foot-long (198.1-meter-long) section of the power plant, along with its eight gigantic generators.

THE CONTROVERSY OVER CHINA'S THREE GORGES DAM

China is currently in the midst of constructing what will be the world's largest dam once it is completed in 2009. This gravity dam will stretch 1 mile (1.6 kilometers) across and reach a height of 600 feet (182.9 meters). Set on the Yangtze River, the Three Gorges Dam, according to Chinese officials, will lessen devastating flooding and (through its hydro-electric power) greatly reduce the pollution currently produced by coal use. Those who oppose the dam's construction, however, point to the 2 million people it will displace as well as the 1,208 historic sites that will be flooded over by the dam's reservoir.

Visitors who want to see still more of the dam can perch themselves on the dam's penstock viewing platform. From here, they can view one of the large penstock pipes that carries voluminous amounts of water from Lake Mead to the power house's generators.

In the Visitor Center, guests can find many exhibits that explain how the dam was built and how it works. One of the newer exhibits, dedicated in 1996, is called "The Bronze Turbine." This exhibit, designed by Kevin Mills and created by Lauri Slenning, is an arrangement of seven bronze relief panels. Matching the dam and power plant's original art deco style, each one depicts the benefits the famous dam has brought to the West.

Lake Mead

Lake Mead is now a part of the Lake Mead National Recreation Area that is run by the National Park Service. Lake Mohave, located downstream from the dam, is also a part of the national recreation area. Attracting more than 9 million visitors each year, the Hoover Dam's reservoir has become one of the most popular vacation and recreation areas in the country, catering to boaters, swimmers, fishing enthusiasts, and sunbathers alike.

When they were completed, the Hoover Dam and Lake Mead *(above)* became two of the most popular tourist attractions in the United States. Standing tall as the eighteenth-highest dam in the world, about 2,000 to 3,000 people visit this engineering wonder every day.

In addition, it continues to serve as a water supply to the western United States and as the source of power for the hydropower plant that serves hundreds of thousands of people. A visitor to Disneyland in Anaheim, California, or a tourist at Sea World in San Diego, California, who drinks from a fountain at either park is actually drinking water from the Colorado River and Lake Mead, 300 miles (482.8 kilometers) away.

The Hoover Bypass Project

United States Highway 93 crosses right over the top of the Hoover Dam and is the shortest route from Las Vegas to eastern locations. This road is also part of the North American Free

Trade Agreement route, which means that it is one of the main commercial routes between Canada and Mexico. It is also the main commercial route between the states of Arizona, Nevada, and Utah. This bypass carries a busy 18,200 vehicles each day—twice the number that it carried 15 years ago.

Traveling on this road is often slow due to traffic congestion and the narrow and curvy roads that make it difficult to navigate. In some spots the road also does not have much of a shoulder, which can pose problems when accidents occur or vehicles break down. The portion of highway near and over the Hoover Dam is potentially dangerous. The sharp curves mean that drivers cannot always see upcoming traffic congestion and may not have enough time to stop to prevent hitting the car in front of them.

The solution to this problem is known as the Hoover Dam Bypass Project. Work on the project's design began in August 2001, and construction is projected to finish in 2010 at a total cost of $240 million. The current road over the dam will remain open while the construction of a new bridge progresses. Once the new bridge is complete, the old road will be used only for dam and Bureau of Reclamation facilities access—not through traffic.

The bridge should prove to be a much easier and quicker route, partly because security checkpoints to ensure the dam's safety will no longer be needed for crossing. Currently, motorists who travel over the dam must stop for vehicle inspections when approaching the dam from either side of U.S. Highway 93. One checkpoint in Nevada lies just 1 mile (1.6 kilometers) north of the dam, and the other checkpoint is located in Arizona, 9 miles (14.5 kilometers) south of the dam.

Because of the dam's immense size, there really is no good way to take a photograph of its front without boarding a helicopter. This situation will change, however, once the Bypass Project is complete. The new bridge spanning the Colorado will provide one of the most scenic photographic sites in the United States and a perfect view of this great dam that encompasses a nation's technological advancement and strong human spirit.

CHRONOLOGY

1776 Spanish priest Francisco Garcés gives the Colorado River its name.

1857 Lieutenant Joseph C. Ives is charged with the job of traveling the Colorado to determine its potential as a shipping route.

1901 People make the first attempt to control the Colorado by diverting its flow; the attempt fails in 1905 when a great flood occurs.

1902 Arthur Powell Davis conceives the idea for a great dam on the Colorado River.

TIMELINE

1902
Arthur Powell Davis conceives the idea for a great dam on the Colorado River

July The U.S. Reclamation Service is established in accordance with the Reclamation Act

1929
June President Hoover signs a proclamation that makes the Boulder Canyon Project Act effective and paves the way for the construction of the Hoover Dam

1902 —————— 1930

1922
November 24 Six states sign the Colorado River Compact, finally putting an end to years of disagreement over water rights and usage in the West

1930
September 17 Secretary of the Interior Ray Lyman Wilbur announces that the Boulder Dam will now be renamed Hoover Dam

1902 *June 17* Congress passes the Reclamation Act to help with water resource issues in the West.

July The U.S. Reclamation Service is established in accordance with the Reclamation Act.

1921 *January* Walker Young leads a Reclamation Service team as part of an official program to test the potential of damming the Colorado.

1922 *November 24* Six states sign the Colorado River Compact, finally putting an end to years of disagreement over water rights and usage in the West.

Congress orders a study on the possible development of the Colorado Basin area.

1931
March 4 The Bureau of Reclamation awards Six Companies the contract to build the Hoover Dam

May 12 Work on the diversion tunnels begins

1936
March 1 The Hoover Dam project is officially complete

1931 **1987**

1933
June 6 Building of the actual dam structure begins when the first bucket of concrete is poured

1987
May 31 The energy produced at the Hoover Dam power plant and sold fully pays for the project's original construction costs

1923   The U.S. Reclamation Service is renamed the Bureau of Reclamation.

The Boulder Canyon Project Act is first introduced in Congress.

1928   *December*   The Swing-Johnson bill passes in Congress and is signed into law by President Calvin Coolidge.

1929   *June 25*   President Herbert Hoover signs a proclamation that makes the Boulder Canyon Project Act effective and paves the way for the construction of the Hoover Dam.

1930   *September 17*   Secretary of the Interior Ray Lyman Wilbur announces that the Boulder Dam will now be renamed Hoover Dam.

1931   *February 19*   Six Companies, the unique group of former individual businesses, becomes an official corporation.

March 4   The Bureau of Reclamation awards Six Companies the contract to build the Hoover Dam.

May 12   Work on the diversion tunnels begins.

1932   *September*   Work begins on the cofferdams that will protect the dam site from possible flooding during construction.

November 14   The Colorado River is successfully rerouted around the work site through the diversion tunnels.

1933   *May 8*   New secretary of the interior Harold Ickes announces that the name of the Hoover Dam will revert back to Boulder Dam.

June 6   Building of the actual dam structure begins when the first bucket of concrete is poured.

1935   *February 6*   The Hoover Dam's final bucket of concrete is poured.

1936   *March 1*   The Hoover Dam project is officially complete.

1941   *August*   The spillways are tested successfully.

1947 *March–April* House Resolution 140 is introduced, passes in Congress, and is signed by President Truman, changing the great dam's name one final time to Hoover Dam.

1983 *Spring* The spillways reduce downstream flooding during an unusually wet season.

1984 Congress passes the Hoover Power Plant Act, which allows for the construction of additional visitor facilities and the Hoover Dam Bypass Bridge.

1987 *May 31* The energy produced at the Hoover Dam power plant and then sold has fully paid for the project's original construction costs.

GLOSSARY

buttress   A support for large structures that props up a wall from its side.

cement   A mixture to which water is added that hardens like rock.

divert   To make something go in a different direction.

embankment   A bank of earth and rock with a flat top and sloping sides.

engineer   A person who designs and builds complicated structures or machines.

erosion   The process of earth elements, such as wind or water, gradually wearing away a structure.

gravity   The natural force that pulls all things to each other.

grout   A paste-like mixture used to fill in spaces that hardens after it is applied.

hydroelectric power   Power for electricity produced by falling or flowing water and a turbine.

intake towers   Tall towers behind a dam that act as a drain.

kilowatt-hours   Units of work or energy equivalent to that done by one kilowatt of power acting for one hour; one kilowatt equals 1,000 watts or 1.34 horsepower.

reservoir   A non-natural lake created behind a dam.

silt   Extremely fine soil carried down a river that settles at its mouth.

spillways   Chutes designed to safely allow excess water from a reservoir to flow over or around a dam.

tributaries   Streams that flow into a larger river.

turbine   A mechanical wheel that uses energy from water or steam to turn a shaft or axle.

"3,000-Year-Old Dam Revives Farming in Turkish Village." Stone Pages: Archaeo News. http://www.stonepages.com/news/archives/002192.html.

"Arthur P. Davis, Director." Bureau of Reclamation. http://www.usbr.gov/history/davis.html.

"The Benefits of Dams to Society." United States Society on Dams. http://www.ussdams.org/ben_new.html.

"Big Dig: Facts & Figures." Massachusetts Turnpike Authority. http://www.masspike.com/bigdig/background/facts.html.

"Big Dig: Project Background." Massachusetts Turnpike Authority. http://www.masspike.com/bigdig/background/index.html.

Billington, David P., and Donald C. Jackson. *Big Dams of the New Deal Era: A Confluence of Engineering and Politics.* Norman: University of Oklahoma Press, 2006.

"Building Big: Dam Basics." PBS. http://www.pbs.org/wgbh/buildingbig/dam/basics.html.

"Bureau of Reclamation: About Us." Bureau of Reclamation. http://www.usbr.gov/main/about.

"The Bureau of Reclamation: A Very Brief History." Bureau of Reclamation. http://www.usbr.gov/history/borhist.html.

Cappato, Jorge. "The International Demand Against Dams Is Growing." United Nations Environment Programme: Global 500 Forum. http://www.global500.org/feature_3.html.

"Cofferdams." Bureau of Reclamation: Lower Colorado Region. http://www.usbr.gov/lc/hooverdam/History/essays/coffer.html.

"Concrete." Bureau of Reclamation: Lower Colorado Region. http://www.usbr.gov/lc/hooverdam/History/essays/concrete.html.

"Cracking Dams." SimScience. http://simscience.org.

"Crossing Hoover Dam: A Guide for Motorists." Bureau of Reclamation: Lower Colorado Region. http://www.usbr.gov/lc/
hooverdam/crossingguide.pdf.

"Declaration of Curitiba: Affirming the Right to Life and Livelihood of People Affected by Dams." RiverNet. http://www.
rivernet.org/general/movement/curitiba.htm.

"Digital Projects: Hoover Dam." University of Las Vegas
Libraries. http://digital.library.unlv.edu/early_las_vegas/
hoover_dam/hoover_dam.html.

"Divided Over Dams." PBS: The American Experience—Hoover
Dam. http://www.pbs.org/wgbh/amex/hoover/sfeature/
damdivided.html.

Dunar, Andrew J., and Dennis McBride. *Building Hoover
Dam: An Oral History of the Great Depression*. New York:
Twayne Publishers, 1993.

Dunn, Andrew. *Dams* (Structures). New York: Thomson Learning, 1993.

Federal Energy Regulatory Commission. "Saluda Dam Remediation: Frequently Asked Questions and Answers." http://www.
ferc.gov/industries/hydropower/safety/projects/saluda/
saluda_qa.pdf.

"The Film & More: Enhanced Transcript." PBS: The American
Experience—Hoover Dam. http://www.pbs.org/wgbh/amex/
hoover/filmmore/transcript/index.html.

"Fortune Magazine: September 1933." Bureau of Reclamation:
Lower Colorado Region. http://www.usbr.gov/lc/hooverdam/
History/articles/fortune1933.html.

"Frequently Asked Questions: The Colorado River." Bureau of
Reclamation: Lower Colorado Region. http://www.usbr.gov/
lc/hooverdam/faqs/riverfaq.html.

"Frequently Asked Questions: The Dam." Bureau of Reclamation: Lower Colorado Region. http://www.usbr.gov/lc/
hooverdam/faqs/damfaqs.html.

"Frequently Asked Questions." Hickory Log Creek Dam and Reservoir Project. http://www.hickorylogcreek.com/faqs.html.

"Frequently Asked Questions: Lake Mead." Bureau of Reclamation: Lower Colorado Region. http://www.usbr.gov/lc/hooverdam/faqs/lakefaqs.html.

"Frequently Asked Questions: Power." Bureau of Reclamation: Lower Colorado Region. http://www.usbr.gov/lc/hooverdam/faqs/powerfaq.html.

"Frequently Asked Questions: Tunnels, Penstocks and Spillways." Bureau of Reclamation: Lower Colorado Region. http://www.usbr.gov/lc/hooverdam/faqs/tunlfaqs.html.

"The Front of Hoover Dam." SunsetCities: Hoover Dam. http://www.sunsetcities.com/hoover-dam/hoover-dam-photos-frontviews.html.

"Herbert Hoover and the Colorado River." Bureau of Reclamation: Lower Colorado Region. http://www.usbr.gov/lc/hooverdam/History/articles/hhoover.html.

"High Scalers." Bureau of Reclamation: Lower Colorado Region. http://www.usbr.gov/lc/hooverdam/History/essays/hscaler.html.

"The Hoover Dam Bypass Project." Hoover Dam Bypass Web Site. http://www.hooverdambypass.org.

"The Hoover Dam Bypass Project." SunsetCities: Hoover Dam. http://www.sunsetcities.com/hoover-dam/bypassproject.html.

"Hoover Dam: Discovery Tour." Bureau of Reclamation: Lower Colorado Region. http://www.usbr.gov/lc/hooverdam/faqs/damfaqs.html.

"Hoover Dam Factoids for Kids." Bureau of Reclamation: Lower Colorado Region. http://www.usbr.gov/lc/hooverdam/educate/kidfacts.html.

"The Hoover Dam Intake Towers." SunsetCities: Hoover Dam. http://www.sunsetcities.com/hoover-dam/hoover-dam-photos-intaketowers.html.

"Hoover Power Plant." Bureau of Reclamation: Lower Colorado Region. http://www.usbr.gov/power/data/sites/hoover/hoover.html.

Hunt, Bernice Kohn. *Dams: Water Tamers of the World.* New York: Parents' Magazine Press, 1977.

Jackson, Donald C. *Building the Ultimate Dam: John S. Eastwood & the Control of Water in the West.* Lawrence: University Press of Kansas, 1995.

"Lower Colorado Dams Office." Bureau of Reclamation: Lower Colorado Region. http://www.usbr.gov/lc/hooverdam/service/DiscoveryTour.html.

"Major John Wesley Powell." John Wesley Powell Memorial Museum. http://www.powellmuseum.org/MajorPowell.html.

McBride, Dennis. "Boulder City History: Miss Vegas." Boulder City Magazine. http://www.bouldercitymagazine.com/past_issues/2007_september/history.html.

McCarney, Kerry J. "Saluda Dam Remediation." The Geological Society of America. http://gsa.confex.com/gsa/2003SC/finalprogram/abstract_49774.htm.

McDonagh, Gavin. "The Dam Dilemma." Riverdeep. http://www.riverdeep.net/current/2001/07/073001_dams.jhtml.

Modern Marvels: Hoover Dam [DVD], A&E Television Networks, 1999.

Oxlade, Chris. *Dams,* 2nd ed. (Building Amazing Structures). Chicago: Heinemann Library, 2006.

"People & Events." PBS: The American Experience—Hoover Dam. http://www.pbs.org/wgbh/amex/hoover/peopleevents.

"Roster of Presidents." American Society of Civil Engineers. http://www.asce.org/150/presidents.html.

"Saluda Backup Dam Named 2006 Outstanding Civil Engineering Achievement." SCANA Corporation. http://www.scana.com/en/news-room/press-releases/archives/2006/SCEG-2006-05-02.htm.

"Santa Ana River Project (SARP): Prado Dam." County of Orange. http://www.ocflood.com/SAR_Prado_Dam.asp.

"Santa Ana River Project (SARP): Seven Oaks Dam." County of Orange. http://www.ocflood.com/SAR_Seven_Oaks_Dam. asp.

Sevastiades, Patra McSharry. *The Hoover Dam* (The Library of American Landmarks). New York: PowerKids Press, 1997.

Smith, Norman. *A History of Dams.* London: Peter Davies, 1971.

"Spillways." Bureau of Reclamation: Lower Colorado Region. http://www.usbr.gov/lc/hooverdam/History/essays/spillways. html.

Stevens, Joseph E. *Hoover Dam: An American Adventure.* Norman: University of Oklahoma Press, 1988.

"Tunnels." Bureau of Reclamation: Lower Colorado Region. http://www.usbr.gov/lc/hooverdam/History/essays/tunnels. html.

"The Visitors Center: 'The Bronze Turbine' Exhibit." SunsetCities: Hoover Dam. http://www.sunsetcities.com/hoover-dam/ hoover-dam-photos-visitorscenter.html.

"Wages." Bureau of Reclamation: Lower Colorado Region. http:// www.usbr.gov/lc/hooverdam/History/essays/wages.html.

"What Is Hydrology and What Do Hydrologists Do?" U.S. Geological Survey: Water Science for Schools. http://ga.water. usgs.gov/edu/hydrology.html.

"What's In a Name?" Bureau of Reclamation: Lower Colorado Region. http://www.usbr.gov/lc/hooverdam/History/essays/ spillways.html.

"Who Builds Big? Interview—Andrew T. Straz." Building Big. http://www.pbs.org/wgbh/buildingbig/profile/interview/ straz.html.

"Wonders of the World Databank—Edwards Dam." Building Big. http://www.pbs.org/wgbh/buildingbig/wonder/structure/ edwards.html.

"Wonders of the World Databank—Three Gorges Dam." Building Big. http://www.pbs.org/wgbh/buildingbig/wonder/structure/ three_gorges.html.

World Commission on Dams. Dams and Development: A New Framework for Decision-Making—Executive Summary. World Commission on Dams. http://www.dams.org/report/execsumm.htm.

FURTHER RESOURCES

BOOKS

Barter, James. *The Colorado* (Rivers of the World). Farmington Hills, MI: Lucent Books, 2003.

Dunar, Andrew J., and Dennis McBride. *Building Hoover Dam: An Oral History of the Great Depression*. New York: Twayne Publishers, 1993.

Dutemple, Lesley A. *The Hoover Dam* (Great Building Feats). Minneapolis, MN: Lerner, 2003.

Hile, Kevin. *Dams and Levees* (Our Environment). Farmington Hills, MI: KidHaven Press, 2007.

Lüsted, Marcia Amidon. *The Hoover Dam* (Building History Series). Farmington Hills, MI: Lucent Books, 2003.

Mann, Elizabeth. *The Hoover Dam: The Story of Hard Times, Tough People, and The Taming of a Wild River* (Wonders of the World Book). New York: Mikaya Press, 2006.

McNeese, Tim. *The Colorado River* (Rivers in American Life and Times). Philadelphia: Chelsea House Publishers, 2004.

WEB SITES

The Boulder City/Hoover Dam Museum
http://www.bcmha.org

Building Big: Dams
http://www.pbs.org/wgbh/buildingbig/dam/index.html

Geoguide: Dams!
http://www.nationalgeographic.com/geoguide/dams

Herbert Hoover Presidential Library and Museum: Hoover Online!
http://www.ecommcode.com/hoover/hooveronline/hoover_dam/toc.html

Nevada History: A Walk in the Past—The Boulder Canyon Project
   AKA Hoover Dam
http://www.nevada-history.org/boulder_canyon_project.html

University of Las Vegas Libraries Digital Projects: Hoover Dam
http://www.library.unlv.edu/early_las_vegas/hoover_dam/
   hoover_dam.html

VIDEOS

American Experience: Hoover Dam [DVD], WGBH Boston,
   2006.
Modern Marvels: Hoover Dam [DVD], A&E Television Networks, 1999.

PICTURE CREDITS

ABOUT THE AUTHOR

REBECCA ALDRIDGE has been a writer and editor for more than 12 years. In addition to this title, she has written several nonfiction children's books, including titles on Thomas Jefferson, Italian immigrants in America, and the *Titanic*. As an editor, she has had input on more than 50 children's books covering such diverse topics as breast cancer, vegetarianism, and tattooing and body piercing. She lives in Minneapolis, Minnesota.